Social Issues
in Literature

Racism in
Maya Angelou's
*I Know Why the
Caged Bird Sings*

Other Books in the Social Issues in Literature Series:

Social Issues
in Literature

Racism in
Maya Angelou's
I Know Why the
Caged Bird Sings

Claudia Johnson, Book Editor

GREENHAVEN PRESS

An imprint of Thomson Gale, a part of The Thomson Corporation

Detroit • New York • San Francisco • New Haven, Conn. • Waterville, Maine • London

Christine Nasso, *Publisher*
Elizabeth Des Chenes, *Managing Editor*

© 2008 The Gale Group.

Star logo is a trademark and Gale and Greenhaven Press are registered trademarks used herein under license.

For more information, contact:
Greenhaven Press
27500 Drake Rd.
Farmington Hills, MI 48331-3535
Or you can visit our Internet site at http://www.gale.com

ISBN-13: 978-0-7377-3901-5 (hardcover)
ISBN-10: 0-7377-3901-0 (hardcover)
ISBN-13: 978-0-7377-3905-3 (pbk.)
ISBN-10: 0-7377-3905-3 (pbk.)

Library of Congress Control Number: 2007937606

Contents

Chapter 3: Contemporary Perspectives on Racism

Introduction

Two of the most influential books in the last half of the twentieth century are set in the 1930s in the South, and they were published when a revolution in race was occurring in the United States. Both of these works are written from a young female's point of view. The difference is that one, Harper Lee's 1960 *To Kill a Mockingbird*, is from a white point of view and the other, Maya Angelou's 1970 *I Know Why the Caged Bird Sings*, is from an African American point of view.

The issue of race in both works, Lee's fiction and Angelou's autobiography, has its origins in black slavery in North America. Until 1865, when the Thirteenth Amendment outlawing slavery was ratified, the economic backbone of the American South rested on the enslavement of black people, and northern industry was buttressed by the raw products, like cotton, that were produced by slave labor.

But for fifty years after the Civil War, the way of life forced on black people was, in many ways, as atrocious as slavery. After they were freed, they had few options to survive: They could leave their plantations for better possibilities in the North; they could remain on the plantations and continue their old lives as freedmen and be recompensed with room, board, and modest wages, which kept them continually in debt to the company store; or they could seek jobs elsewhere doing arduous, dangerous work, primarily for railroad companies and other new industries. Contracts bound black men to these companies for decades.

Many employers, looking to take advantage of the large groups of ex-slaves looking for work on the streets of small towns, prompted the passage of strict laws calling for the arrest of these unemployed black men as vagrants. Then, as convict labor, the ex-slaves were forced to do grueling work without pay as their sentences were extended.

Although slavery and some of the extreme exploitation of workers (like the vagrancy laws and convict labor) was eventually made illegal, much from the past—good and bad—persisted during Angelou's childhood. Common African ancestry and the travails that isolated black people from the predominant white society led to a black culture which was, as Angelou describes it, the backbone and consolation that held black society and individuals together. Angelou describes some of those cultural entities in her book, including the strongest adhesion in the communities—the African American church.

Many ex-slaves did leave the South, flooding into cities like the District of Columbia, Detroit, New York, St. Louis, Philadelphia, and Chicago searching for jobs and a better life in general. On one hand, moving out of the South broadened the experiences of African Americans and fulfilled their dreams for better lives. On the other hand, children were usually left behind with relatives. The end result was the breakup of families. Young Angelou and her brother, Bailey, were left behind with their grandmother. It was not unusual for children to go for months or even years without seeing or even hearing from their parents.

In many ways, available work for black men and women changed little in the early twentieth century. During the 1930s, the setting of Angelou's novel, and for four or five decades later black men were excluded from any job of leadership or management, from blue-collar jobs, and from any but the lowest form of physical labor. Typically, in small towns, as Harper Lee suggests in *To Kill a Mockingbird*, black men were restricted to the lowest jobs on farms and in lumber mills. In the public sector, the only jobs available were those of garbage men. Of course, the backbreaking work of cotton picking, especially in the South, was a job that was always available. Angelou describes in her book the painful effect this work had on people. Black women, in towns like Angelou's childhood home of Stamps, Arkansas, were overwhelmingly restricted to work in the fields, housework, cooking, and babysitting. Angelou's grandmother is an astonishing exception in that she ran her own store.

The boundary between the black and white parts of Stamps, Arkansas, was so rigid that Angelou rarely saw a white person. There was segregation of schools, restaurants, hotels, churches, swimming pools, restrooms, and stores. Angelou was once turned away by a local white dentist who refused to treat her.

Most frightening for blacks during this period was the real threat of lynching. And most self-destructive was the endless humiliation by whites.

The writers of the following articles discuss in-depth the issues of race that emerge in Maya Angelou's *I Know Why the Caged Bird Sings*, her first autobiography.

Chronology

1928

Marguerite Johnson, who would later change her name to Maya Angelou, is born April 4 in St. Louis.

1931

Marguerite is sent to Stamps, Arkansas, with her brother to live with her grandmother, Annie Johnson Henderson, whom the children call "Momma."

1935

Marguerite's father takes the children back to St. Louis to live with their mother.

1936

Marguerite is raped by her mother's boyfriend, who is subsequently murdered by Marguerite's relatives.

1937

Both children are returned to Stamps, Arkansas, and their "Momma."

1940

Marguerite graduates with honors from Lafayette County Training School.

1941

Marguerite moves to San Francisco to live with her mother.

1942

Marguerite goes to night school at the California Labor School.

1944
Marguerite becomes the first black female trolley car conductor. She graduates from Mission High School, and her son, Guy, is born.

1949
Marguerite marries Tosh Angelos.

1953
Marguerite divorces Tosh Angelos and changes her name to Maya Angelou.

1954
Angelou performs at the Purple Onion in San Francisco and tours in other plays for three years.

1961–1966
Angelou works as a journalist in Cairo, Egypt, and as a dramatist and musician in Ghana, Africa.

1966
Angelou returns to Los Angeles, California, as a lecturer and performer.

1970
Angelou publishes *I Know Why the Caged Bird Sings* and works as writer in residence at the University of Kansas and Yale University.

1974
Angelou publishes her second autobiographical work, *Gather Together in My Name*.

1976
Angelou publishes her third autobiographical work, *Singin' and Swingin' and Gettin' Merry Like Christmas*.

1981

Angelou publishes her fourth autobiographical novel, *The Heart of a Woman*. She is given a lifetime appointment as Reynolds Professor of American Studies at Wake Forest University in North Carolina.

1986

Angelou publishes her fifth autobiographical work, *All God's Children Need Traveling Shoes*.

1993

Angelou becomes the first black woman to compose and read a poem at a presidential inauguration (for Bill Clinton).

2002

Angelou publishes her sixth autobiographical work, *A Song Flung Up to Heaven*.

Background on Maya Angelou

The Life of Maya Angelou

Lynn Z. Bloom

Lynn Z. Bloom, a faculty member at the University of Connecticut and a scholar of William Faulkner and composition, also authored Dr. Spock: Bibliography of a Conservative Radical *and* The Seven Deadly Virtues and Other Lively Essays.

Maya Angelou's first autobiography, I Know Why the Caged Bird Sings, *is not just the story of her life in a small town in the South. It is a rare piece of social history of the time and a look at the lives of all African Americans as they faced the painful continuation of slave mentality and discrimination.*

Angelou's beloved grandmother gave her love and security after her parents abandoned her. She was later raped by her mother's boyfriend. Even though her early life was a struggle, Angelou was able to escape the plantation mentality of the South and see that a larger world existed.

Maya Angelou's literary significance rests upon her exceptional ability to tell her life story as both a human being and a black American woman in the twentieth century. Four serial autobiographical volumes have been published to date (in 1970, 1974, 1976, and 1981), covering the period from 1928 to the mid-1960s; more may be expected. She asserts in *I Know Why the Caged Bird Sings* (1970): "The fact that the adult American Negro female emerges a formidable character is often met with amazement, distaste and even belligerence. It is seldom accepted as an inevitable outcome of the struggle won by survivors and deserves respect if not enthusiastic acceptance." And yet, Angelou's own autobiographies and vivid lectures about herself, ranging in tone from warmly humorous to bitterly satiric, have won a popular and critical following that is both respectful and enthusiastic.

Lynn Z. Bloom, from *Afro-American Writers After 1955: Dramatists and Prose Writers.* Farmington Hills, MI: Gale Research Company, 1985. Copyright © 1985 Gale Research Company. Reproduced by permission of Gale, a part of Cengage Learning.

An Interpreter of Black Culture

As she adds successive volumes to her life story, she is performing for contemporary black American women—and men, too—many of the same functions that escaped slave Frederick Douglass performed for his nineteenth-century peers through his autobiographical writings and lectures. Both become articulators of the nature and validity of a collective heritage as they interpret the particulars of a culture for a wide audience of whites as well as blacks; as one critic said, Angelou illuminates "with the intensity of lightning the tragedy that was once this nation's two-track culture." As people who have lived varied and vigorous lives, they embody the quintessential experiences of their race and culture.

An account of the life and major writings of Maya Angelou is of necessity based largely on information that she herself has supplied in her autobiographies; where lacunae exist, they do so because Angelou herself has chosen not to discuss certain periods of time, events, or people. . . .

Angelou's odyssey—psychological, spiritual, literary, as well as geographical—begins with *I Know Why the Caged Bird Sings*, generally acceded to be the best of her four autobiographical volumes and the exclusive focus, to date, of serious critical attention. Marguerite Johnson (she did not become Maya Angelou until her debut as a dancer at the Purple Onion cabaret in her early twenties) was born in St. Louis on 4 April 1928 to Bailey and Vivian Baxter Johnson. When she was three and her brother Bailey was four, they were sent by their divorced parents to live in Stamps, Arkansas, which was, she said, the same as "Chitlin' Switch, Georgia; Hang 'Em High, Alabama; Don't Let the Sun Set on You Here, Nigger, Mississippi." "High spots in Stamps were usually negative," she observes, "droughts, floods, lynchings and deaths."

There Angelou remained for a decade, reared by her maternal grandmother, Annie ("Momma") Henderson, who kept a country store and ruled her grandchildren with the same sense of "work, duty, religion," and morality with which she ruled her own life. Observes Angelou, "I don't think she ever knew that a deep-brooding love hung over everything she touched."

In Stamps Angelou learned what it was like to be a black girl in a world whose boundaries were set by whites. She learned what it meant to wear for Easter a "plain ugly cut-down [dress] from a white woman's once-was-purple throw-away," her skinny legs "greased with Blue Seal Vaseline and powdered with the Arkansas red clay." As a young child she expected at any minute to wake from "my black ugly dream" and find her "Nappy black hair" metamorphosed to a long, blonde bob. She thought, then, that "God was white," but wondered whether He would "allow His only Son to mix with this crowd of cotton pickers and maids, washerwomen and handymen." She learned the humiliation of being refused treatment by a white dentist who would "'rather stick my hand in a dog's mouth than in a nigger's.'"

But she learned, also, that blacks would not only endure, but prevail. Momma, head of one of the few black families "not on relief" during the Depression, was an honest but shrewd businesswoman who could turn aside the taunts of the "powhitetrash" and beat the bigoted dentist at his own game. From her Angelou learned common sense, practicality, and the ability to control one's own destiny that comes from constant hard work and courage, "grace under pressure." She learned, sometimes forcibly, the literature of black writers: "Bailey and I decided to memorize a scene from *The Merchant of Venice*, but we realized that Momma would question us about the author and that we'd have to tell her that Shakespeare was white, and it wouldn't matter to her whether he was dead or not. So we chose 'The Creation' by James Weldon Johnson instead."

But the pride in herself this new knowledge engendered took a devastating fall when she was eight, during a brief stay in St. Louis with her beautiful mother, Vivian Baxter, "light-skinned with straight hair." She was raped by her mother's boyfriend, a taciturn "big brown bear" who was found "dropped . . . [or] kicked to death" shortly afterward. In court she had not revealed that she had permitted him to fondle her on two earlier occasions. Therefore she felt responsible for his murder (committed by her uncles), and she decided that "I had to stop talking."

Back in Stamps, where she was sent perhaps because "the St. Louis family just got fed up with my grim presence," her bourgeoning pride disappeared for nearly five years, along with her speech. Both were restored by delicious afternoons, "sweet-milk fresh" memory, of reading and reciting the world's great literature with Mrs. Flowers, the educated "aristocrat of Black Stamps" who "acted just as refined as whitefolks in the movies and books and . . . was more beautiful"; "she made me proud to be a Negro, just by being herself."

She learned during this time the importance of self-expression, as well as communication, for "the wonderful, beautiful Negro race" survives "in exact relationship to the dedication of our poets (include preachers, musicians and blues singers)." She explained to an interviewer in 1981 that "there isn't one day since I was raped that I haven't thought about it . . . I have gotten beyond hate and fear, but there is something beyond that." Her multiple careers in the arts—singing, dancing, and writing—have become ways of transcending her personal hates and fears, as well as of proclaiming her black identity and pride.

In 1940, after Angelou's graduation at the top of her eighth grade, her fun-loving mother, now a professional gambler, moved the children from Stamps to San Francisco, imposing experience on innocence, disorder upon order. Maya's subsequent formal education consisted of attending George Washington High School in San Francisco throughout World War II, while concurrently taking dance and drama lessons at the

Maya Angelou displays a copy of I Know Why the Caged Bird Sings *in 1971.* AP Images.

California Labor School. Her informal schooling, in the "fourteen-room typical San Franciscan post-Earthquake" rooming house her mother ran in the Fillmore District, was much more extensive. From her mother she learned "proper posture, table manners, good restaurants"; from her stepfather, how to play "poker, blackjack, tonk and high, low, Jick, Jack and the Game"; from the household, the ways of shipyard workers, "much-powdered prostitutes," and "the most colorful characters in the Black underground."

These people she accepted as honest in their own way. But she fled the hypocrisy of a summer vacation with her failed father and his nouveau bourgeois girl friend in their tacky trailer in southern California. Unable to return to her mother for a month, she lived in a graveyard of wrecked cars, many inhabited by homeless children whose own natural brotherhood "set a tone of tolerance for my life."

The book ends with her determined rush toward maturity. With the perseverance that foreshadowed later civil rights work, she finally obtained a job, while still in high school, as the first black woman streetcar conductor in San Francisco. With equal determination to prove that she was a woman, she became pregnant and at sixteen was delivered of a son one month after graduation from Mission High School's summer school in 1945. She has since been awarded honorary degrees by Smith College, Mills College, and Lawrence University, among others.

The next installment of Angelou's autobiography, *Gather Together in My Name* (1974), seems much less satisfactory than the first. This may be in large part because here Angelou is less admirable as a central character than she was in *I Know Why the Caged Bird Sings*. Here, in instance after instance, she abandons or jeopardizes the maturity, honesty, and intuitive good judgment toward which she had been moving in *Caged Bird....*

Learning to Be Proud

In *The Heart of a Woman* (1981) Angelou intertwines an account of seven years of her own coming of age (1957–1963) with the coming of age of the civil rights movement and the beginning of the women's movement. Her enlarged focus and clear vision transcend the particulars and give this book a fascinating universality of perspective and psychological depth that almost matches the quality of *I Know Why the Caged Bird Sings* (in contrast to the shallower and more limited intervening volumes). Its motifs are commitment and betrayal.

By the time she was thirty, Angelou had made a commitment to become a writer. Inspired by her friendship with the distinguished social activist author John Killens, she moved to Brooklyn to be near him and to learn her craft. . . .

At the same time Angelou made a commitment to promote black civil rights. Her widening circle of black intellectual friends was "persistently examining the nature of racial oppression, racial progress and racial integration," excoriating "white men, white women, white children and white history, particularly as is applied to black people." Through Killens and others she learned to acknowledge her kinship with blacks nationwide. . . .

So when she met Martin Luther King she was prepared to accept his challenge: "We, the black people, the most displaced, the poorest, the most maligned and scourged, we had the glorious task of reclaiming the soul and saving the honor of the country." With comedian Godfrey Cambridge she organized a benefit, "Cabaret of Freedom," for King's Southern Christian Leadership Conference [SCLC]. She was starring "on the stage of life" a "general in the army" of fighters against legal discrimination, and as a consequence was soon appointed by the veteran civil rights activist, Bayard Rustin, to succeed him as the SCLC's northern coordinator. During her six months in office she was grateful for the interracial cooperation that was "new and old and dynamic," from children to adults alike, not only in Harlem but throughout the nation. The same dynamism pervaded the black support of communists, from [dictator Fidel] Castro's Cuba to Russia. Angelou vividly captures the mood of the era with snatches of song, dialogue, and slogans that dynamically punctuate this book: "Castro never had called himself white, so he was O.K. from the git . . . and as black people often said . . . 'Wasn't no Communist lynched my poppa or raped my mamma.' 'Hey, [Soviet Union premier Nikita] Khruschev. Go on, with your bad self.'" . . .

The Search for Identity

In describing her development in her autobiographies, Angelou gives generous credit to the influences of *dominant women* during her childhood. *I Know Why the Caged Bird Sings* focuses on three impressive female role models: "Momma" Henderson, her powerful, enterprising, righteous, religious grandmother; Mrs. Flowers, beautiful, cultivated, and pridefully black; and her mother, the sexy, sassy, and savvy embodiment of black mores. The combined characteristics of these women became leitmotifs throughout the volumes of Angelou's autobiography.

Men, however, get little credit for who she is and how she got that way. During Angelou's childhood adult black men were either absent (her father), weak (her crippled uncle), subservient to women (her uncle and her mother's boyfriends), sexually abusive (the man who raped her), or lazy and hedonistic (her father when she met him again in her teenage years). Of the men she has romantic relationships with as an adult (to the point at which *Heart of a Woman* ends), the blacks are either stodgy (her bail bondsman fiancé) or unwilling to make a long-term commitment (Make). The man who treats her with greatest respect and affection is white (Angelos, her first husband).

But the primary disruptive factor in all these relationships is Angelou's quest for self-identity, manifested through self-assertiveness and the self-expression that come not only from her careers as a dancer, a singer, and a writer, but from being very good at these endeavors. As she matures, she becomes more and more her own person. Through her own efforts and innate talent, which she minimizes in concentrating on the results, she succeeds early and spectacularly in these highly competitive fields in which many fail. Her enjoyment of the freedom, mobility, independence, and acclaim that success makes possible is evident from the zestful assurance with which she writes her autobiographies. . . .

Because she continues to write, a final critical assessment of her work would at this point [1985] be premature. Yet it is clear from the four-volume serial autobiography that Angelou is in the process of becoming a self-created Everywoman. In a literature and a culture where there are many fewer exemplary lives of women than of men, black or white, Angelou's autobiographical self, as it matures through successive volumes, is gradually assuming that exemplary stature. . . .

Angelou's autobiographical volumes explain both why she is worth being looked at and why, like many blacks, both real and fictional, she "didn't come to stay" but is always moving on. For she is forever impelled by the restlessness for change and new realms to conquer that is the essence of the creative artist, and of exemplary American lives, white and black.

The Life That Shaped the Book and the Book That Shaped the Life

Joanne M. Braxton

Joanne M. Braxton, a professor of American Studies and English at the College of William and Mary and a scholar of African American women's literature, is also the editor of The Collected Poetry of Paul Laurence Dunbar.

Maya Angelou rose from humble beginnings and severe psychological trauma to a position of impressive leadership in race relations. In her best-known book, I Know Why the Caged Bird Sings, *she looks back in anger at the racism and rape she suffered as a child.*

Maya Angelou employs two voices to tell her story: that of a young girl, searching for an identity and trying to survive, and the now-accomplished adult, narrating the tale of a young black girl growing up in the South in the early twentieth century.

Maya Angelou, Z. Smith Reynolds Professor of American Studies at Wake Forest University in Winston-Salem, North Carolina, is the author of five autobiographies, of which *I Know Why the Caged Bird Sings* (1970) is the first and best known. Even before accepting the lifetime appointment at Wake Forest, Angelou's teaching and experience spanned not only the United States and Europe but also Africa and the Middle East.

A Life of Leadership

A celebrated poet, teacher, and lecturer who has taught at the University of California, the University of Kansas, and the University of Ghana, among other places, Angelou has been

Joanne M. Braxton, "Symbolic Geography and Psychic Landscapes," *Maya Angelou's* I Know Why the Caged Bird Sings. New York: Oxford University Press, 1999, pp. 3–20. Reproduced by permission of Oxford University Press.

honored for her academic and humanistic contributions as a Rockefeller Foundation Scholar and a Yale University Fellow. While in Ghana, she worked for the *African Review* as feature editor. Previously, while residing in Cairo, Egypt, Angelou (who speaks French, Spanish, and Fanti) edited the *Arab Observer*.

In the 1960s Angelou served as northern coordinator of the Southern Christian Leadership Conference at the invitation of Dr. Martin Luther King. She has received presidential appointments from President Gerald Ford, who asked her to serve on the U.S. Bicentennial Commission, and President Jimmy Carter, who appointed her to the National Commission on the Observance of International Women's Year. A member of the original cast of Jean Genet's *Les Blancs*, as well as the European touring company of *Porgy and Bess*, Angelou's acting credits include an Emmy Award–nominated performance as Kunte Kinte's grandmother in the televised film version of Alex Haley's *Roots*.

Without a doubt, Maya Angelou is America's most visible black woman autobiographer. While black women writers might share traditional motivations for writing autobiography, other motives derive from their unique experiences. In the eyes of the predominantly white and male culture, women, and particularly black women, speak as "others," which is to say that, at least as far as the awareness of the dominant group is concerned, the black woman speaks from a position of marginality. And yet, against all odds, she comes to self-awareness and finds herself at the center of her own experience. Veiled though she might be (even twice veiled, thrice if she should be a member of a sexual minority), the black woman autobiographer possesses her own self-conscious vision of herself and her community. She sees herself and her community in relation to those who have described her as "other," and the very awareness of her enforced marginality becomes an additional catalyst for life writing, for testifying, for "telling it like it is."

Anger in Looking Back

Often masked, the anger of the black woman autobiographer is a deep and abiding one, as must inevitably be the case when an "othered" writer develops enough awareness of self and self-esteem to believe that her life is worth writing about. "When I pick up the pen to write," Angelou told Bill Moyers in a PBS interview, "I have to scrape it across those scars to sharpen the point."

Maya Angelou has tempered her own anger and put it to a constructive purpose; her work speaks to the necessity of reflecting, remembering, opening, cleansing, healing, and, at times, issuing a warning. In *I Know Why the Caged Bird Sings*, she focuses almost entirely on the inner spaces of her emotional and personal life, crafting a "literary" autobiography that becomes not merely a personal record but also a stage on which the sins of the past can be recalled and rituals of healing and reconciliation enacted.

As I have suggested elsewhere, *Caged Bird* "is perhaps the most aesthetically satisfying autobiography written by a black woman in the years immediately following the Civil Rights era." Since its initial publication almost thirty years ago, *I Know Why the Caged Bird Sings* has continually ranked on the *New York Times*' Best Seller List. *Caged Bird* has been studied by many critics; it still resonates, even with readers generations beyond its original audience. And Angelou's audience has increased along with her public stature. The *New York Times* reported that "the week after Angelou's recitation of 'On the Pulse of the Morning' at the 1993 inauguration of President William Jefferson Clinton, *Caged Bird*'s sales increased by nearly 500 percent, forcing Bantam to reprint approximately 400,000 copies of the autobiography and Angelou's other works."

Although *Caged Bird* has generated a substantial body of criticism and found a solid place in the humanities curriculum, it is not a book that has been received without controversy. According to Lyman B. Hagan, "*I Know Why the Caged*

Maya Angelou recites a poem at the inauguration of President Bill Clinton in 1993. AP Images.

Bird Sings, lauded by many as a literary classic which should be read and taught to all African American young people, is one of the ten books most frequently targeted for exclusion from high school and junior high school libraries and class-rooms." Why? Poet and critic Opal Moore puts it this way: "*Caged Bird* elicits criticism for its honest depiction of rape, its exploration of the ugly spectre of racism in America, its re-counting of the circumstances of Angelou's own out-of-wedlock teen pregnancy, and its humorous poking at the foibles of the institutional church. Angelou inscribes her resis-tance to racism, sexism, and poverty within the language, the imagery, the very meaning of her text; her truth-telling vision confronts stereotypes old and new, revising perspective and discomforting the reader seeking safety in the conventional platitudes of the status quo. Simultaneously, *Caged Bird*'s pro-foundly moral stance challenges its audience to confront the contradictions of life and to create positive change, beginning with one's self and then one's community. As such, the task that Angelou set out for herself as a writer must be acknowl-edged as one of exceeding complexity; she seeks to inspire and to direct."

Two Voices and Memories

Angelou employs two distinct voices in *Caged Bird*, that of the mature narrator and that of the girlchild whom Angelou calls "the Maya character" (and whom I call Marguerite). . . .

Taken together, the two voices might be seen as represent-ing the interplay of history and memory. To borrow from the blues idiom of [novelist] Ralph Ellison, the mature autobiog-rapher consciously fingers the jagged edges of her remem-bered experience, squeezing out a tough lyric of black and blue triumph. Maya Angelou, née Marguerite Johnson, emerges miraculously through a baptismal cataract of vio-lence, abuse, and neglect. Evoking transcendent awareness through the agency of memory, the *symbolic* Maya Angelou rises to become a "point of consciousness" for her readers. In *I Know Why the Caged Bird Sings*, the reader might hear echoes of [Russian writer Maksim] Gorky or [Russian novelist Fyodor] Dostoyevsky, [American writer] Zora Neale Hurston or [American novelist] Richard Wright, yet Angelou signifies on these inherited models to "sing" her sassy song of the self. . . .

Critics of fiction and nonfiction alike agree that memory is a "plastic" medium through which the past can be seen and reconstructed. "[M]emory is almost sacred," wrote French historian Pierre Nora. And Melvin Dixon saw memory as a tool that could be used both to dismantle and reclaim. In his words, "Memory becomes a tool to regain and reconstruct not just the past but history itself." Putting it another way, critic and writer Karen Fields wrote, "[M]emory collaborates with forces separate from actual past events, such as an individual's wishes, a moment's connotations, an environment's clues, an emotion's demands, a self's evolution, a mind's manufacture of order, and yes, even a researcher's demands." Toi Derricotte expressed it simply and more elegantly, perhaps, when she wrote, "Memory is in the service of the greatest psychic need. . . ."

Who is the "phenomenal woman" known as Maya Angelou (née Marguerite Johnson)? "Dr. Angelou" to her students and colleagues at Wake Forest University, "Dr. A." to her staff, "Sister" to her colleague and friend Professor Dolly McPherson, "Aunty" to her niece Rosa Johnson, and "Grandmother" to her beloved grandson Colin Ashanti Murphy Johnson. Like the little girl Marguerite whom she has somehow kept alive within her memory and her spirit all of these years, Angelou has continued to grow, returning continually to the black experience for models and inspiration.

Social Issues in Literature

CHAPTER 2

I Know Why the Caged Bird Sings and Racism

Metaphors of a Racial Struggle

Joan Didion

Joan Didion is an expert photographer, journalist, and writer of fiction and nonfiction. Her latest work, staged on Broadway, is The Year of Magical Thinking.

Events and episodes of racial rejection take on symbolic value in I Know Why the Caged Bird Sings. As a child, Angelou felt like an outcast in white society—disparaged for her appearance and race, symbols of "otherness." However, symbols of cruelty are not only white but black, such as a mother, who symbolizes abandonment and carelessness, and a black rapist, who represents brutality.

Angelou's novel itself is symbolic of a slave narrative, a recollection of a former slave of his or her struggle from bondage to liberty. In her journey, Angelou overcomes violence and racism to become an accomplished author, poet, actress, filmmaker, and lecturer.

I *Know Why the Caged Bird Sings* is the first and still best-loved volume in [Maya Angelou's] autobiographical series. *Caged Bird* begins with a symbolic prelude concerning Maya's fears of being stared at in church. Her emotions in this introductory section focus on her contempt for her black skin; like Pecola Breedlove in Toni Morrison's *The Bluest Eye*, she wishes for the privileges that come with being white. . . . This opening incident [is] one of several in which Maya feels abused and devalued because she is a black child who perceives herself as the "other" in a white world. Her "black ugly dream" introduces a motif which sets up the theme of racial displacement that occupies much of *Caged Bird* and of the subsequent volume, *Gather Together in My Name.* . . .

Mothers

Throughout much of *Caged Bird* Maya remains displaced, rejected in a racist society and all but abandoned by her mother, Vivian Baxter. In one of several reflective fantasies, the child imagines her mother lying in a coffin, dead, faceless: "since I couldn't fill in the features I printed M O T H E R across the O, and tears would fall down my cheeks like warm milk." The empty face of the mother is perceived through the imagination of a child who prints, who writes, who stares back. In the gap left by the absent mother Maya erects Momma Henderson: "I saw only her power and strength. She was taller than any woman in my personal world, and her hands were so large they could span my head from ear to ear."

I Know Why the Caged Bird Sings abounds in such moments of verbal force, where the metaphors perfectly correspond to the emotion, as in Momma's encompassing hands, as in the Christmas misery when Maya destroys the blond-haired doll her mother had sent her but preserves the other gift, a tea set, "because any day or night she might come riding up." The doll and the tea set seem to represent Maya's torn self, the angry child versus the ungrateful child—the doll destroyed in anger but the tea set saved in the hope of Vivian's return. . . .

Angelou presents a similar death of the spirit in describing her visit, with Momma, to a white dentist who would rather put his "hand in a dog's mouth than in a nigger's." The horrendous equation between "dog" and "nigger" recounts the history of dehumanization recorded by African American writers, from the first slave narratives to the "mad and hungry dogs" of Claude McKay's famous sonnet, "If We Must Die." Humiliated for herself, for her grandmother, for her culture,

Maya retaliates silently in a fantasy of power where Momma's eyes burn "like live coals" and her arms grow to twice their length.

The most powerful emotional response in the first autobiography, however, is Maya's negation of speech after being raped during a stay with her mother in St. Louis. The beautiful Vivian has a lover, Mr. Freeman, who befriends Maya and later rapes her. Angelou describes the episode in language that has been broadly acclaimed for its candor:

> Then there was the pain. A breaking and entering when even the senses are torn apart. The act of rape on an eight-year-old body is a matter of the needle giving because the camel can't. The child gives, because the body can, and the mind of the violator cannot.

After the rape Maya, ill from the shock and from the pain, is sent to the hospital, where she tells Bailey the rapist's identity. Mr. Freeman is tried and found guilty but inexplicably released the very day of his sentencing. Not long afterward Mr. Freeman's corpse is found behind a slaughterhouse, apparently kicked to death. Although the text suggests that Maya's uncles and grandmother were involved in Mr. Freeman's murder, this is never stated explicitly. After the trial and subsequent murder Maya, who has lied about her earlier sexual contact with Mr. Freeman, becomes mute so that the "poison" in her breath will not damage anyone else. Like Momma in the "powhite trash" episode, the victimized child experiences a self-imposed "perfect silence."

Abandoned, Displaced, and Saved

Vivian Baxter, unable to charm her daughter into speech, sends both children back to Arkansas. Once again in the sanctuary of her grandmother's general store, Maya gathers strength from the African American community, whose values of self-determination and personal dignity help her to overcome her muteness. Maya gains special strength from Bailey and from Mrs. Bertha Flowers, a genteel black woman whose passion for reading helps Maya recover her speech—although Angelou, in a 1990 interview with Dolly McPherson, admitted that her "voluntary mutism" actually lasted "almost five years." Maya is eventually restored to speech, regaining her language through self-education and through formal training. Despite her crisis, Maya is able to graduate with top honors from the Lafayette County Training School in Stamps. Four years later she graduates from George Washington, a predominantly white high school in San Francisco, where she studies under Miss Kirwin, a "rare educator who was in love with information" and who had no "teacher's pets." While still in high school she receives a scholarship to study dance and theater at the California Labor School, also called the Mission School. Maya nonetheless remains insecure about her sexuality, so damaged has she been from the psychological consequences of the rape and the ensuing trial and murder. She develops negative images about her body; she thinks that her large bones, small breasts, and deep voice indicate that she is a lesbian. In order to disprove this notion she seduces a handsome neighborhood boy and becomes pregnant. At the end of *I Know Why the Caged Bird Sings*, Maya is a single mother, yet still herself a child, a mother afraid she might harm her baby. Maya's mother, Vivian Baxter, assuages this fear by firmly placing the infant in her daughter's arms. . . .

Parallels with Slave Narratives

The slave narrative in its earliest form was the recollection by a former slave of her or his struggles in the journey from Africa to America and, once in America, from bondage to liberation. Many of these narratives were oral, translated into written words through the sponsorship of a white benefactor, although some narratives, written by slaves, celebrate the achievement of literacy as a major theme. (Frederick Douglass' *Narrative*, for example). William L. Andrews, an authority on

the antebellum slave narrative, stresses the connection between freedom and literacy: "In the slave narrative the quest is
toward freedom from physical bondage and the enlightenment
that literacy can offer to the restricted self- and social consciousness of the slave."

Like the slave narrative, Angelou's autobiographies are informed by the motif of the journey and its opportunities for
enlightenment. Her quest takes her from ignorance to consciousness, from muteness to articulation, from racial bondage
to liberation.

Fear, Lies, Silence, and Singing

Elizabeth Fox-Genovese

Elizabeth Fox-Genovese is the Eleanor Rail Professor of Humanities and director of women's studies at Emory University. She has written widely on feminism and slavery, including The Mind of the Master Class *(2005).*

In I Know Why the Cage Bird Sings, *Maya Angelou writes of the deception and silence necessary for survival. In Stamps, Arkansas, everyone, especially blacks, knows his or her place. Marguerite longs for whiteness: white skin, straight blond hair, decent clothes, respect, and simple recognition.*

To probe her identity, to stop lying about herself to cover her fear, Angelou turns to her pen to atone for past falsities and to acknowledge the truth about herself. To do this she must leave the South behind and reexamine the racial traditions in which she has been reared.

Slavery days are long gone, but their traces linger, shooting up like those uncontrollable weeds that can eat up a garden in the course of a summer. Even during slavery, free black communities flourished in the North and in pockets of the South. But the very name "free black" belies those communities' freedom from the heavy hand of slavery as a social system and indexes their ties to the South. The tradition of African-American autobiography began, in [author] William L. Andrews's phrase, as the determination "to tell a free story." The obsession with freedom betokened the indissoluble, if submerged, obsession with slavery. Race grounded the association. In a country in which only black people were enslaved, blackness and unfreedom merged in a shadowy nega-

Elizabeth Fox-Genovese, "Myth and History: Discourse of Origins in Zora Neale Hurston and Maya Angelou," *Black American Literature Forum*, vol. 24, summer 1990, pp. 221–235. Reproduced by permission of the author.

tion of the virtues of freedom. Slavery grounded and guaranteed racism. Slavery confirmed the association between freedom and virtue, between freedom and whiteness, between whiteness and virtue. Slavery negated the individualism of blacks singly, negated the autonomy of blacks as a community. And these very negations ineluctably bound "free" blacks to the history of their enslaved brothers and sisters. In dissociating themselves from the condition of their enslaved people, they risked dissociating themselves from their people—from their race. . . .

A Tight Web

Gender, race, and condition wove a tight web around black women's possibilities for self-representation, especially since for them, as for their men, any understanding of the self led back over dusty roads to Southern cages. Worse, the conventions of womanhood that whites had developed and middle-class blacks apparently embraced branded the very act of authorship as pushy and unfeminine. As women and as blacks, African-American women autobiographers were, in some measure, bound to construct their self-representations through available discourses, and in interaction with intended readers. For them, as for white women and for white and black men, the self had to be represented in the (recognizable) discourses of one or more interpretive communities. To be sure, their self-representations could variously—and even simultaneously—comply with, subvert, or transform prevailing discourses. But the abiding danger persisted of seeing themselves through the prism of a (white) androcentric discourse, literally through men's eyes, through white eyes. . . .

In different ways, Zora Neale Hurston [author of *Dust Tracks on a Road*] and Maya Angelou broke ground for new representations of the African-American female self. *Dust Tracks*, published in 1942, and *Caged Bird*, published in 1969, explicitly reclaim the Southern past as the grounding of their authors' identities. Both explicitly reject white norms of womanhood as models. In Hurston's pages, the Southern past re-emerges as a mythic past suitable for the unique self; in Angelou's pages, it acquires a historical and sociological specificity that helps to account for the modern strength of the female self as survivor.

Angelou thus opens *Caged Bird* under the aegis of memory, truth, and passing through. The "n[o]t stay[ing]" of the poem recited by the children in the Colored Methodist Episcopal Church in Stamps, Arkansas, referred to the reality of resurrection from the brevity and immateriality of life on this troubled earth to a better life. Yet in Angelou's hands, the poem also evokes a secular meaning. Surely, her younger self had not come to Stamps to stay. Was she not merely passing time before rejoining her parents, claiming her birthright, embarking on a better life?

For the young Marguerite, the birthright she would one day claim is her own whiteness. Watching her grandmother make her dress for that Easter day, she had known "that once I put it on I'd look like a movie star," would "look like one of the sweet little white girls who were everybody's dream of what was right with the world." But the light of Easter morning harshly reveals the magic dress to be only "a plain ugly cut-down from a white woman's once-was-purple throwaway." Yet Marguerite clings to the truth of her own resurrection: "Wouldn't they be surprised when one day I woke out of my black ugly dream . . .?" It was all a dreadful mistake. "Because I was really white and because a cruel fairy stepmother, who was understandably jealous of my beauty, had turned me into a too-big Negro girl, with nappy black hair, broad feet and a space between her teeth that would hold a number two pencil." And Angelou, the narrator, notes, bringing her adult knowledge to bear on the memories, "If growing up is painful for the Southern Black girl, being aware of her displacement is the rust on the razor that threatens the throat. It is an unnecessary insult."

In *Caged Bird*, Angelou sifts through the pain to reappropriate—on her own terms—that Southern past and to undo the displacement. Her highly crafted, incandescent text selectively explores the intertwining relations of origins and memory to her identity. The unrecognized whiteness of the child she represents herself as having been gives way to the proud blackness of the woman she has become. The pride is the pride of a survivor, of history repossessed. That "the adult American Negro female emerges a formidable character," she insists, should be "accepted as an inevitable outcome of the struggle won by survivors."

In her brief opening prologue, Angelou establishes both her perspective as adult narrator—the survivor of the memories of which she is writing—and the perspective of the child she recollects herself as having been. As child she presumably experienced the world around her in a seamless flow, punctuated by disconnected fragments, like a young girl's traumatic inability to control her urine. The adult narrator captures the emblematic memories, vivid and compelling in themselves, and weaves them together to illustrate and anchor the truth of the story as a whole. The prologue thus offers a concrete identification of the protagonist as black, Southern female—the interpreter of her own experience, the teller of her own story. . . .

Shortly after graduation [of Marguerite from the eighth grade], Momma [Marguerite and Bailey's grandmother] decides that Marguerite and Bailey are to join their mother in California. Stamps is no place for an ambitious black boy, no place, although she never says so, for an ambitious black girl. Marguerite's previous trip away from Stamps, her previous stay with her mother, offered no grounds for believing that the world beyond Stamps is safer. During that stay in Saint

Louis, Marguerite had been raped by the man with whom her mother was living. Withal, Angelou does not represent that rape, which racked the eight-year-old girl's body with unbearable pain, as the worst. The worst occurred during the subsequent trial of the rapist at which Marguerite, forced to testify, lied. Under examination she felt compelled to say that Mr. Freeman had never tried to touch her before the rape, although he had and she believed she had encouraged him to. That lie "lumped in my throat and I couldn't get air." On the basis of that lie Mr. Freeman was convicted. In fact, the lie did not cause Mr. Freeman to serve time; his lawyer got him released. It did cause his death. No sooner had he been released than her mother's brothers killed him. To Marguerite, "a man was dead because I lied. . . . Obviously I had forfeited my place in heaven forever. . . . I could feel the evilness flowing through my body and waiting, pent up, to rush off my tongue if I tried to open my mouth. I clamped my teeth shut, I'd hold it in."

The Enlightenment of Mrs. Flowers

In the wake of the trial, Marguerite and Bailey were sent back to Stamps, where for nearly a year Marguerite persisted in her silence. Then, Mrs. Bertha Flowers, "the aristocrat of Black Stamps," threw her a life line. Mrs. Flowers "was one of the few gentlewomen I have ever known, and has remained throughout my life the measure of what a human being can be." From the start, Mrs. Flowers appealed to her because she was like "women in English novels who walked the moors (whatever they were) with their loyal dogs racing at a respectful distance." Above all, "she made me proud to be a Negro, just by being herself." Mrs. Flowers joined the world of Stamps to the world of literature, embodied in her person the dreams that shaped Marguerite's imagination. For Marguerite, under Mrs. Flowers's tutelage, formal education became salvation. But even as she introduced Marguerite to the delights of *Tale of Two Cities*, Mrs. Flowers enjoined her to recognize the beauties and sense of black folk culture. Ignorance and illiteracy, she insisted, should not be confused. "She encouraged me to listen carefully to what country people call mother wit. That in those homely sayings was couched the collective wisdom of generations."

Language, the human form of communication, alone separate man from the lower animals. Words, she insisted, have a life beyond the printed page. Words, even written words, acquire meaning by being spoken. Books should be read aloud. Angelou thus represents Mrs. Flowers as bridging the gap between oral and literary culture, between the black community of Stamps and *Jane Eyre*. Under Mrs. Flowers's influence, Marguerite again began to speak....

The South's Lies

It all comes back to the South. But it also comes back to lies. For Hurston, lying represented the magic of men's tales, the delights of crafted deception, even if, on her own telling, lying also masked fear. No less than Hurston, Angelou recognized lying as the mask of fear, but for her lying led not to stories but to imposed silence. To write her story—to speak at all— she had to conquer the fear, repudiate the lie. Hurston's South instructed her in the necessity of lying to preserve the self from violence, denial, and death, but in her glorious "lies" she denied the knowledge, transformed the fearful reality into a death-defying myth. To be heard at all she felt obliged to represent herself in black face—a spoofing, harmless minstrel. The lessons of Angelou's South were no less harsh, but including as they did the faith of Momma, the courage of Henry Reed [a classmate], and the teachings of Mrs. Flowers, they also taught her that the South need not be wrapped in mythical denial. It could be claimed as the legacy of the people— especially the women—who had taught her how to survive and to sing.

Race and Education

Fred Lee Hord

Fred Lee Hord is director of the African American Cultural Center at North Carolina State. His books include Reconstructing Memory: Black Literary Criticism *and* I am Because We Are: Readings in Black Philosophy.

A sense of placelessness contributes to Marguerite's feeling of worthlessness. No one wants her, so she is shifted from town to town. Among other things, books save her. Here she has friends and companions, and she can identify with heroes and heroines. Her real life heroes are champion heavyweight boxer Joe Louis, called the strongest man in the world, and her father, whose sophistication and command of English allow him to hold his own with Marguerite's school principal. Her epiphany comes when she realizes that black educators and parents value athletics over academics.

[Maya Angelou's *I Know Why the Caged Bird Sings*] traces her development from a girl of three in Stamps, Arkansas to a woman of almost seventeen with a baby boy in San Francisco, California. And it is the early development of a black female "Invictus" who is becoming the master of her fate and the captain of her soul by the end of this phase of her life. She is discovering who she is in spite of the forms of masculine prejudice, white illogical hate and black lack of power with which she has been besieged. The most critical masculine prejudice with which she was confronted was that in the eyes of black boys—eyes persuaded by young minds already affected by the colonizer's definitions that hourglass figures were the only ones with which to pass the time of day, and that fair skin, straight hair, a slender nose and thin lips were requisites for beauty. And though she is not yet in favor with her own eyes by the time she brings two more male eyes into the world, she is not obsessed with looking like white girls. The illogical hate of whites was ripe in Stamps and real in San Francisco, but she has refused to accommodate the power reverberations of that hate. Albeit she lived with black lack of power, it has not possessed her being. She has accepted neither whites controlling the lives of African-Americans nor African-Americans surrendering theirs. Thus, from a narrow crack in that small southern town and an ostensibly wider one in that large western city—St. Louis, Los Angeles and Mexico in between—she wedged a space, someplace to be a black girl. Marguerite Johnson—even though the painful process of maturation for a black girl in the South was intensified by her awareness that she had been assigned a place of no place—inevitably created a "place to be somebody," for she was a survivor.

To discover how Marguerite created someplace to be a black girl, we shall examine how she took the book world she gained access to and superimposed it on the overlapping yet distant black and white worlds in Stamps. Further, we shall analyze how she increasingly expanded the world she integrated from those first three by using the expanding space of societal permission and societal contact in her experience after Stamps. Marguerite "always, but ever and ever, thought that life was just one great risk for the living," and so took risks, disguised and open ones, in order to be. The freedom of the book world was too sweet not to transfer to the breathing ones.

Literature as Place

Although Marguerite had already located the book world in print, it was Mrs. Bertha Flowers who set it securely on the axis of human communication. With the real world run by whites—a world with scarce black-white contact, much less communication—Mrs. Flowers' revelation that books could be rounded into a Third World provided a place much more livable than Stamps. Marguerite explains the meaning of the secret world furnished by Mrs. Flowers:

> To be allowed, no, invited, into the private lives of strangers and to share their joys and fears, was chance to exchange the Southern bitter wormwood for a cup of mead with Beowolf or a hot cup of tea and milk with Oliver Twist.

The book world was a world of integration, where you were the confidant of all the denizens—in whose skins, regardless of color, you could move inside and breathe free. Yes, the black [authors Paul] Dunbar, [Langston] Hughes, [James Weldon] Johnson and [W.E.B.] DuBois lived in that world, but so did the white [authors William] Shakespeare, [Rudyard] Kipling, [Edgar Allan] Poe, [Samuel] Butler, [William Makepeace] Thackeray, and [William Ernest] Henley. She saved her "young and loyal passion" for the black writers, but she discovered ways to enjoy the company of white writers who related to her real world. It "was Shakespeare who said, 'When in disgrace with fortune and men's eyes,'" a condition she identified with when she thought about her plight in Stamps, a young castaway without parents in a freedom-stifling, small southern town. The statement also fit her estimate of herself in the eyes of people, especially young black boys. Shakespeare sympathized with the "black, ugly dream" that was her existence, and so became her "first white love." She rationalized her courtship "by saying that after all he had been dead so long it couldn't matter to anyone any more." The "beautiful sad lines" of "Annabel Lee" appertained to the sadness of her life "stalled by the South and Southern Black lifestyle." And whether it was the comic strips, cowboy books or Horatio Alger, she craved another space, a place to be a happy black girl. The freedom of the cowboys, "the strong heroes who always conquered in the end," and the penniless shoeshine boys who, with goodness and perseverance, became rich, rich men and gave baskets of goodies to the poor on holidays, became more real than the people in her haltingly moving space. [Musician] Tiny Tim was her favorite on "Sunday as he eluded the evil men and bounded back from each seeming defeat as sweet and gentle as ever." As she daydreamed herself into fortune and the grace of men's eyes, she identified with "the little princesses who were mistaken for maids, and the long-lost children mistaken for waifs." Marguerite refused to restrict her life to the world of the cotton fields; like her father, Bailey Sr., she had "aspirations of grandeur." And it was this survivor spirit that impelled her to turn her mind fast enough to occupy a less confining globe.

Only Athletics

Marguerite Johnson banished segregation in her book world, and she wanted no part of her culture that she associated with powerlessness in the world of book learning. Considered stuck-up by her schoolmates, she took pride in the school principal's proper English and tailored her speech accordingly, speech free of what she considered the rough edges of a "Southern accent" or "common slang." In fact, one of her most traumatic experiences was graduation from the eighth grade at Lafayette County Training School. The long anticipated event was ruined by a combination of the white arrogance of the commencement speaker, Mr. Donleavy, and the apparent acceptance by African-Americans in the audience that they could only aspire to be great athletes. Education was supposed to be the exit out of the stultifying South, and now a white man was saying that they should try to emulate only the "Jesse Owenses [Olympic gold medalist in track and field] and Joe Louises [champion heavyweight boxer]" Enraged by the presumptuousness and rebutting each sentence, she wondered "what school official in the white-goddom of Little Rock had the right to decide that these two men must be our only heroes." Further, she willed instant death to the black owner of the first Amen, hoping that he/she would choke on the word. She also considered the recitation of "Invictus" by Elouise, the daughter of the Baptist minister, impertinent, and was aggravated by Henry Reed's valedictory address, "To Be or Not to Be." If according to Mr. Donleavy—who represented all whites—African-Americans could not be, and Whites were the masters of their fate and the captain of their souls, then commencement was just another exercise in futility. "We were maids and farmers, handymen and washerwomen, and anything higher that we aspired to was farcical and presumptuous." If education was not a way out of the strictures of the Stamps in this country, then democracy was a sham, and all the people, black and white, who were regarded as contributors to that cause, had lived in vain. It would have been preferable for everyone to have died than continue to play out this "ancient tragedy" of white power and black impotence. Marguerite summarizes the feelings that characterized her attitude about being denied self-determination. . . .

Some Power of Their Own

All of the black people that she admired possessed some degree of freedom from whites. Momma Johnson, her grandmother, owned a store which whites patronized, owned land and houses, and "had more money than all the powhitetrash." In fact, she lent money to whites, including the dentist, during the Depression. Marguerite "knew that there were a number of white folks in town that owed her favors." So Momma was a black woman to look up to, who not only was "the only Negro woman in Stamps referred to once as Mrs."—though by error—but who also asserted herself and won strange victories over both poor white girls and a rich white man—the dentist.

In the store, Momma sidestepped servility with the "powhitetrash girls" by anticipating their needs and thus obviating their orders. Outside the store on one memorable occasion, she was heckled by the girls but stood her ground quietly with the moan-song of old black Christian warriors in her throat even when they subjected her to the indignity of indignities—having one of their gang expose her genitals by doing a handstand without underwear. Even though Marguerite could not fathom why her grandmother did not come inside to avoid such humiliation, she realized, after the ordeal, that "whatever the contest had been out front ... Momma had won."

Momma also won the bout with Dentist Lincoln, who had never treated a black patient. She pleaded with him to extract two of Marguerite's teeth, reminding him that she had once lent him money, but he refused, saying that he would rather stick his "hand in a dog's mouth than a nigger's." Marguerite remembered how she had been dismissed by Momma, and how she had imagined a scene between Momma and the dentist and his nurse. In that scene, Momma, with "well enunciated" words, castigated the dentist, ordered him out of Stamps, relegated him to a veterinarian, and refused to waste the energy to kill him. When leaving, "she waved her handkerchief at the nurse and turned her into a crocus sack of chicken feed." ...

Her Heroes

Joe Louis, the Brown Bomber, wore a black face, and held the fists of almost all black people in his hands when he stepped into the ring to not only defend his heavyweight championship but his people. Marguerite was one of his people, one of the black ritual participants in the late Thirties on the nights of the Louis fights. She remembered how the community gathered and waited on the radio to bring the news of another Louis victory—a black victory. And it wasn't only [Italian boxer Primo] Carnera on the canvass; it was all white people. And then Marguerite was proud to belong to her people, because Joe Louis was the "champion of the world. A

Black boy. Some Black mother's son . . . the strongest man in the world." So Marguerite belonged to the strongest people in the world, at least for a while.

Marguerite carried other black heroes on the shoulders of her mind when they seemed to live free of white clutches. When Bailey Sr., her father, came to Stamps, she was "so proud of him it was hard to wait for the gossip to get around that he was in town." Why? He spoke "proper English, like the school principal, and even better. . . . Every one could tell from the way he talked and from the car (De Soto) and clothes that he was rich and maybe had a castle out in California." Marguerite needed exemplars of what she considered freedom to believe in the possibility of her own. Although, as we shall see, she became more secure in her identity as her real world expanded beyond Stamps, she was thrilled by the fact that her uncles in St. Louis whipped whites as well as African-Americans and that the black underground men in San Francisco made fortunes from "the wealthy bigoted whites, and in every case . . . used the victims' prejudice against them." . . .

Marguerite never accepted the occlusions of her place as a black girl in the white South. In thought, word and deed, she pushed against them, making soft spots and then fissures. When "the used-to-be sheriff" rode up to the store late one day and warned Momma to hide Uncle Willie, because the Klan would be by later to avenge the behavior of "a crazy nigger (who) messed with a white lady today," Marguerite pledged that not even St. Peter would secure a testimony from her that the act had been kind. She detested "his confidence that my uncle and every other Black man who heard of the Klan's coming ride would scurry under their houses to hide in chicken droppings." When the "powhitetrash children," who did not obey the customary laws of being respectful, "took liberties in my store that I would never dare," she pinched them, "partly out of angry frustration." Marguerite's experiences in St. Louis with "the numbers runners, gamblers, lottery takers and whiskey salesmen" waiting in the living room of her mother's mother for favors, and with the Syrian brothers at Louie's tavern competing for her mother's attention because she approximated white beauty standards, were sources of new models of black female strength for her return to Stamps as well as of reinforced mystification about her appearance. And so she was more likely than ever to resist the violations of her space as a human being, although she was only able to shift her center of gravity regarding her beauty from white to high yellow. Thus later in Stamps, when she worked in the kitchen of a white woman, Mrs. Viola Cullinan, who insisted on abbreviating her name to Mary, Marguerite reacted to being "called out of her name" by dropping Mrs. Cullinan's favorite dishware, "a casserole shaped like a fish and the green glass coffee cups. Yet, when watching a Kay Francis movie from the Negro balcony, she not only dismissed the obsequious behavior of Kay's black maid and chauffeur as beneath her dignity, but she answered the white laughter at such behavior with her own, reveling in the fact of 'white folks' not knowing that the woman they were adoring could be my mother's twin, except that she was white and my mother was prettier."

Momma's Positive Lessons

Sidonie Ann Smith

Sidonie Ann Smith, of Wayne State University, is the author of Poetics of Women's Autobiography *and* De-Colonizing the Subject: The Politics of Gender in Women's Autobiography.

I Know Why the Caged Bird Sings *opens with a scene in a church. Everyone is looking at Marguerite not because she is black, but because her poverty necessitates that she wear a made-over, faded dress. In society at large, however, she not only had the wrong dress, but also the wrong hair and the wrong face and the wrong legs. She was the wrong color. And the response she gets causes her to ask herself, over and over again in her mind, "What you looking at me for?"*

A young, awkward girl child, dressed in a cut-down faded purple, too-long taffeta gown, stands nervously before an Easter congregation in Stamps, Arkansas, asking, "What you looking at me for?" The next lines refuse to escape forgetfulness, imprinting this one indelibly on the shame-filled silence. Finally the minister's wife offers her the forgotten lines. She grabs them, spills them into the congregation and then stumbles out of the watching church, "a green persimmon caught between [her] legs." Unable to control the pressure of her physical response, she urinates, then laughs "from the knowledge that [she] wouldn't die from a busted head."

But the cathartic laughter never even begins to mute, much less transcend, the real pain that is this experience, the palpable pain that pulses through her long trip down the aisle of that singing church as urine flows mockingly down her grotesquely skinny, heavily dusted legs. "What you looking at me

Sidonie Ann Smith, "The Song of a Caged Bird: Maya Angelou's Quest after Self-Acceptance," *Southern Humanities Review*, vol. vii, fall 1973, pp. 365–375. Copyright © 1973 by Auburn University. Reproduced by permission.

for?" The question's physical articulation is barely audible; its emotional articulation wails insufferably through the child's whole being, wails her self-consciousness, wails her diminished self-image: "What you looking at me for?"—"What you looking at *me* for?"—over and over until it becomes, "Is something *wrong* with me?" For this child too much is wrong.

The whole way she looks is wrong. She knows it too. That's why they are all looking at her. Earlier as she watches her grandmother make over the white woman's faded dress she revels for one infinitely delicious moment in fantasies of stardom. In a beautiful dress she would be transformed into a beautiful movie star: "I was going to look like one of the sweet little white girls who were everybody's dream of what was right with the world." But between the taffeta insubstantiality of her ideal vision of herself and the raw (fleshy) edges of her substantiality stands the one-way mirror. . . .

Wrong dress. Wrong legs. Wrong hair. Wrong face. Wrong color. Wrong. Wrong. Wrong. The child lives a "black ugly dream," or rather nightmare. But since this life is only a dream, the child knows she will awaken soon into a rightened, a whitened reality. . . .

In a society attuned to white standards of physical beauty, the black girl child cries herself to sleep at night to the tune of her own inadequacy. At least she can gain temporary respite in the impossible dreams of whiteness. Here in the darkened nights of the imagination, that refuge from society and the mirror, blossoms an ideal self. Yet even the imagination is sometimes not so much a refuge as it is a prison in which the dreamer becomes even more inescapably possessed by the nightmare since the very self he fantasizes conforms perfectly to society's prerequisites. The cage door jangles shut around the child's question: "What you looking at me for?" . . .

In Black American autobiography the opening almost invariably re-creates the environment of enslavement from which the black self seeks escape. Such an environment was literal in the earliest form of black autobiography, the slave narrative, which traced the flight of the slave northward from slavery into full humanity. In later autobiography, however, the literal enslavement is replaced by more subtle forms of economic, historical, psychological, and spiritual imprisonment from which the black self still seeks an escape route to a "North." Maya Angelou's opening calls to mind the primal experience which opens Richard Wright's *Black Boy*. Young Richard, prevented from playing outside because of his sick, "white"-faced grandmother, puts fire to curtains and burns down the house. For this his mother beats him nearly to death. Richard's childhood needs for self-expression culminate in destruction, foreshadowing the dilemma the autobiographer discovers in his subsequent experience. His needs for self-actualization when blocked eventuate in violence. But any attempt at self-actualization is inevitably blocked by society, black and white, which threatens him with harsh punishment, possibly even death. Finally Wright is forced to flee the South altogether with only the knowledge of the power of the word to carry with him. *Black Boy*'s opening scene of childhood rebellion against domestic oppression distils the essence of Wright's struggle to free himself from social oppression.

Maya Angelou's autobiography, like Wright's, opens with a primal childhood scene that brings into focus the nature of the imprisoning environment from which the self will seek escape. The black girl child is trapped within the cage of her own diminished self-image around which interlock the bars of natural and social forces. The oppression of natural forces, of physical appearance and processes, foists a self-consciousness on all young girls who must grow from children into women. Hair is too thin or stringy or mousy or nappy. Legs are too fat, too thin, too bony, the knees too bowed. Hips are too wide or not wide enough. Breasts grow too fast or not at all. The self-critical process is incessant, a driving demon. But in the black girl child's experience these natural bars are rein-

Joe Louis stands over Primo Carnera after knocking him to the mat during a 1935 bout. Angelou vividly describes listening to the fight in I Know Why the Caged Bird Sings. *AP Images.*

forced with the rusted iron social bars of racial subordination and impotence. Being born black is itself a liability in a world ruled by white standards of beauty which imprison the child *a priori* in a cage of ugliness: "What you looking at me for?" This really isn't me. I'm white with long blond hair and blue eyes, with pretty pink skin and straight hair, with a delicate mouth. I'm my own mistake. I haven't dreamed myself hard enough. I'll try again. The black and blue bruises of the soul multiply and compound as the caged bird flings herself against these bars. . . .

Constant Displacement

Warmth but distance: displacement. The aura of personal displacement is counterpointed by the ambience of displacement within the larger black community. The black community of Stamps [Arkansas] is itself caged in the social reality of racial subordination and impotence. The cotton pickers must face an empty bag every morning, an empty will every night, knowing all along that the season would end as it had begun— money-less, credit-less.

The undercurrent of social displacement, the fragility of the sense of belonging, are evidenced in the intrusion of white reality. Poor white trash humiliate Momma as she stands erect before them singing a hymn. Uncle Willie hides deep in the potato barrel the night the sheriff warns them that white men ride after black, any black. The white apparition haunts the life of Stamps, Arkansas, always present though not always visible. . . .

Nevertheless, there is a containedness in this environment called Stamps, a containedness which controls the girl child's sense of displacement, the containedness of a safe way of life, a hard way of life, but a known way of life. The child doesn't want to fit here, but it shapes her to it. And although she is lonely, although she suffers from her feelings of ugliness and abandonment, the strength of Momma's arms contains some of that loneliness. . . .

In Stamps the way of life remained rigid, in San Francisco it ran fluid. Maya had been on the move when she entered Stamps and thus could not settle into its rigid way of life. She chose to remain an outsider, and in so doing, chose not to allow her personality to become rigid. The fluidity of the new environment matched the fluidity of her emotional, physical, and psychological life. She could feel in place in an environment where everyone and everything seemed out-of-place. . . .

Even more significant than the total displacement of San Francisco is Maya's trip to Mexico with her father. The older autobiographer, in giving form to her past experience, discovers that this "moment" was central to her process of growth. Maya accompanies her father to a small Mexican town where he proceeds to get obliviously drunk, leaving her with the responsibility of getting them back to Los Angeles. But she has never before driven a car. For the first time, Maya finds herself totally in control of her fate. Such total control contrasts vividly to her earlier recognition in Stamps that she as a Negro had no control over her fate. Here she is alone with that fate. And although the drive culminates in an accident, she triumphs.

Humor as a Tool for Survival

Lyman B. Hagen

Lyman B. Hagen, of Butte College, is the author of many articles and books.

The title of Maya Angelou's book, I Know Why the Caged Bird Sings, *suggests that both slaves and caged birds still find the spirit within themselves to sing. Some of those songs, like Angelou's, are expressions of outrage against white society. Angelou, in telling her story, often uses humor to make her painful past palatable for the reader.*

The book's title [*I Know Why the Caged Bird Sings*] cleverly attracts readers while subtly reminding of the possibility of losing control or being denied freedom. Slaves and caged birds chirp their spirituals and flail against their constrictions. . . .

The stories, anecdotes, and jokes in *Caged Bird* do tell a dismaying story of white dominance, but *Caged Bird* in fact indicts nearly all of white society: American men, sheriffs, white con artists, white politicians, "crackers," uppity white women, white-trash children, all are targets. Their collective actions precipitate an outpouring of resentment from the African-American perspective. This suggests a thesis for examining *Caged Bird* through the lens of folklore and humor. It identifies the far broader picture of black America than its depicted focus. . . .

As of the mid 1980s, *Caged Bird* had gone through twenty hardback printings and thirty-two printings in paperback. Angelou's appearance at the 1993 Presidential Inauguration

Lyman B. Hagen, from *Heart of a Woman, Mind of a Writer, and Soul of a Poet: A Critical Analysis of the Writings of Maya Angelou*. Lanham, MD: University Press of America, 1997. Copyright © 1997 by University Press of America, Inc. All rights reserved. Reproduced by permission.

sent the book back to the top of the *New York Times* best seller lists and resulted in another round of printings. In fact, *Caged Bird* has never been out of print since first issued, nor it seems have any of her other books. That *Caged Bird* was once a selection of the Book of the Month Club, the Ebony Book Club, and also nominated for the National Book Award testifies to its appeal and broad popularity. *Caged Bird* alone would assure Angelou a place amongst America's most popular authors. . . .

Humor and the Caged Bird

In *I Know Why the Caged Bird Sings*, Angelou acknowledges that many strong memories of her childhood were of unpleasant happenings. However, she knows what a good solid sense of humor can contribute to the success of stories, and relies on her humor to soften her recollections. Making the difficult palatable allows for the incorporation of subtle judgments on the inequities of black, communal life. Thus while the comedy in *Caged Bird* and in her other writings is often dark humor emerging from hurt, it is woven into her narratives to do more than lighten them. Angelou's mother, Vivian, on a car ride to San Francisco, "strung humorous stories along the road like a bright wash and tried to captivate us." This bridging with humor by Vivian attempts to close the gap caused by her rather haphazard record of mothering. The many jokes, stories, anecdotes, and amusing incidents in Angelou's writings testify to a native humor and its bonding effect. Outsiders feel like insiders when they chuckle and smile together. . . .

Pursuit of Knowledge

The pursuit of knowledge in Angelou's early development, according to [author] George E. Kent, draws on "two areas of black life: the religious and the blues traditions." Her grandmother represents the religious influence: Black Fundamentalism, the Christian Methodist Episcopal (CME) Church. Her mother, on the other hand, stands for the "blues-street tradition," the fast life. Francoise Lionnet-McCumber in her dissertation adds a third term to this comparison: "the literary tradition, all the fictional works that the narrator reads avidly." . . .

Following Angelou's re-awakening and emergence under the guidance of her mentor, Mrs. Flowers, *Caged Bird*'s narrative moves forward, incorporating stories that show what it is to be black in the American South. Angelou's rural family associations are typical of the time and place. She tells of an ecumenical church revival meeting that reflects the religious cooperation and involvement of the entire community. Familiar evening entertainments often revolved around ghost stories which were told to both skeptical and supportive superstitious listeners. . . . Other reports of daily activities reflect life for African Americans in Stamps, Arkansas and the hundreds of other Stamps. . . .

Males in the Novel

In Jungian archetypal terms [doctrine of psychologist and psychiatrist Carl Gustave Jung], Angelou is the anima [the feminine side of personality]. The animus—the male part of her make-up—is represented by her brother Bailey. Bailey Johnson, Jr. is a firm, rather free-spirited youngster who because of being male, is able to move about in his segregated world with fewer restrictions than sister Maya. The two children are very close, probably because of their life situations as much as from their shared experiences and interests. They are both highly literate and adaptable. Bailey is protective of Maya, yet each appears to be very independent. Bailey must face greater dangers in the larger white-dominated world and is taught early on of the risks of being an African-American man. He does not allow this to prevent his functioning as a typical bright, energetic boy. He, more than any other character, with his outgoing personality and natural curiosity seems

A crowd stands beneath two victims of a 1930 lynching in Indiana. Murderous lynchings were the ultimate expression of white domination over African Americans during Angelou's youth. Hulton Archive/Getty Images.

to exemplify Angelou's contention regarding blacks and whites: that they are more alike than un-alike; that there are more similarities than differences Bailey likes reading, comic books, movies, sportscasts, following around his St. Louis uncles and a little strutting. He idolizes his attractive, devil-may-care mother. All of these things could be said about any boy of his age. However, the promise of Bailey the boy seems to have been blunted for Bailey the man who wound up in prison. This is a sad, unfortunate development, but is not openly attributed to race. His embracing the street-style is accepted as a matter of circumstance and choice. . . .

Self-Discovery

In *Caged Bird* and her other autobiographies, Angelou does discover herself and her capabilities and effectively conveys her personality and opinions. Her real purpose in *Caged Bird*, however, as well as in her other books, is to illuminate and explain her race's condition by protesting against white misconceptions and legitimatizing the extremes sometimes required for survival. While justifying some questionable activities, she does not judge the right or wrong of them. She wants to destroy those stereotyped images of African Americans that prevailed when she wrote *Caged Bird*. Angelou rightly resents this thinking that dehumanized her people, and which continued to be practiced despite civil rights progress. Instead of writing an argumentative response or preaching to protest, Angelou chose the traditional form of autobiography to dramatize the conditions, presenting easily understood counter-examples. The reader can relate and conclude that the stereotype image is false and destructive. Forces beyond control dictate actions determined to be anti-social. Given equal opportunities, Angelou believes that like reactions would be demonstrated by blacks and whites. . . .

The Maya character in *Caged Bird* addressed the author's stated themes by overcoming many obstacles, establishing some sense of self as a mother, and repeatedly emphasizing the importance of literacy and education. She also serves the traditional black autobiographical themes of bondage, her dependence on others; flight, as she breaks out on her own with the junk yard group; and freedom, by taking control of her life. Thus Angelou includes all required elements in *Caged Bird* and uses it as the base for her future books.

Seeing African American Women in a New Way

Sondra O'Neale

Sondra O'Neale, a professor at Wayne State University, is the author of Jupiter Hammon and the Biblical Beginnings of African American Literature *(1993).*

I Know Why the Caged Bird Sings *was one of the first books to challenge the common stereotypes of black women, such as the poor woman on food stamps, the young unmarried mother, the mammy, and the prostitute. It portrays black women as strong, smart, resourceful, and independent, particularly Momma Henderson.*

The Black woman is America's favorite unconfessed symbol. She is the nation's archetype for unwed mothers, welfare checks, and food stamps. Her round, smiling face bordered by the proverbial red bandanna is the requisite sales image for synthetic pancakes and frozen waffles "just like Mammy use to make." Only her knowledgeable smile of expertise can authenticate the flavor of corporately fried chicken. When sciolists [amateurs] have need to politicize reactionary measures, they usually fabricate self-serving perceptions of "universal" Black women: ostensibly trading poverty vouchers for mink-strewn Cadillacs, or hugging domestic accouterments in poses of beneficent penury, or shaking a firm bodice as a prostituting Lilith, who offers the most exquisite forbidden sex—all cosmologically craved images of a remote, ambivalent Mother Earth. Regardless of which polemic prevails, these mirrors of the same perverted icon provide the greatest reservoir of exploitable and subconsciously desired meaning in American culture.

The Unknown Black Woman

That said, if the larger society does not know who Black women are, only who it wants them to be; if even Black men as scholars and thinkers writing in this century could not "free" the images of Black women in the national psyche, it remained for Black women to accomplish the task themselves. Thus the emergence of Black feminine expression in drama, poetry, and fiction during the seventies was long overdue. Because ebony women occupy so much space on the bottom rung in American polls of economy, opportunity, and Eurocultural measurements of femininity, some of these new writers know that for Black liberation art must do more than serve its own form, that fictional conceptions of depth and integrity are needed to reveal the Black women's identity, and that ethnic women readers are bereft of role models who can inspire a way of escape.

Although Black writers have used autobiography to achieve these ends since the days of slavery, few use the genre today. One who employs only the tools of fiction but not its "make-believe" form to remold these perceptions, one who has made her life her message and whose message to all aspiring Black women is the reconstruction of her experiential "self," is Maya Angelou. With the wide public and critical reception of *I Know Why the Caged Bird Sings* in the early seventies, Angelou bridged the gap between life and art, a step that is essential if Black women are to be deservedly credited with the mammoth and creative feat of noneffacing survival. Critics could not dismiss her work as so much "folksy" proganda because her narrative was held together by controlled techniques of artistic fiction as well as by a historic-sociological study of Black feminine images seldom if ever viewed in American literature.

No Black women in the world of Angelou's books are losers. She is the third generation of brilliantly resourceful females, who conquered oppression's stereotypical maladies without conforming to its expectations of behavior. Thus, reflecting what Western critics are discovering is the focal point of laudable autobiographical literature, the creative thread which weaves Angelou's tapestry is not herself as central subject; it is rather a purposeful composite of a multifaceted "I" who is: (1) an indivisible offspring of those dauntless familial women about whom she writes; (2) an archetypal "self" demonstrating the trials, rejections, and endurances which so many Black women share; and (3) a representative of that collective obsidian army which stepped out of three hundred years of molding history and redirected its own destiny. The process of her autobiography is not a singular statement of individual egotism but an exultant explorative revelation that she *is* because her life is an inextricable part of the misunderstood reality of who Black people and Black women truly are. That "self" is the model which she holds before Black women and that is the unheralded chronicle of actualization which she wants to include in the canon of Black American literature.

In *Caged Bird*, one gets a rare literary glimpse of those glamorous chignoned Black women of the twenties and thirties who, refusing to bury their beauty beneath maid trays in segregated Hollywood films or New York's budding but racist fashion industry, adapted their alluring qualities to the exciting, lucrative streetlife that thrived in the Jazz Age during the first third of this century. Buzzing with undertones of settlement of the Black urban North and West, these were the days of open gambling, speakeasies, and political bossism. Angelou's mother and maternal grandmother grandly supported their families in these St. Louis and San Francisco environments in ways that cannot be viewed as disreputable because they were among the few tools afforded Black folk for urban survival. But other than nostalgic mention of performing headliners such as [big-band leader] Duke Ellington or [jazz singer] Billie Holiday, one does not get a sense of Black life in literary

This movie theater in Leland, Mississippi, was segregated at the time this photo was taken, in 1939. Hulton Archive/Getty Images.

or historic reconstructions of the era. Truthful assessment would show that most Blacks were not poor waifs lining soup kitchen doors during the Depression or, because they were denied jobs in the early years of the war effort, pining away in secondary involvement. The landscape in *Caged Bird* is not that of boardinghouse living among middle-class whites as depicted through eyes of nineteenth-century Howellian boredom, but rather that of colorful and adventurous group living in San Francisco's Fillmore district during the shipbuilding years of World War II. . . .

The African American Mother

If there is one enduring misrepresentation in American literature it is the Black Southern matriarch. When Blacks appeared first in James Fenimore Cooper's novel *The Spy*, the Black woman was silent, postforty, corpulent, and in the kitchen. Cooper's contemporary, Washington Irving, duplicated that perspective, and for much of the period that followed, white

American authors more or less kept her in that state. By modern times, given characters such as [William] Faulkner's Molly and Dilsey, the images of nonmulatto Southern Black women had still not progressed. When seen at all they were powerless pawns related only to contexts of white aspirations. But Angelou's depiction of her paternal Grandmother Annie Henderson is a singular repudiation of that refraction. While Mrs. Henderson is dependent on no one, the entire Stamps community is at times totally dependent upon her, not as a pietous but impotent weeping post but as a materially resourceful entrepreneur. When explaining that her family heritage precludes acceptance of welfare, Angelou describes Mrs. Henderson's self-sufficiency. . . .

Through frugal but nonarrogant management of her finances under the meddlesome eye of jealous and avaricious whites, Mrs. Henderson not only stalwartly provides for her crippled son and two robust grandchildren, she feeds the Black community during the Depression *and* helps keep the white economy from collapse. Angelou aptly contrasts gratitude and its absence from both segments. While holding the reluctant hand of her granddaughter Maya, who was suffering from a painful abcessed tooth, Grandmother Henderson endured contemptuous rejection from the town's white dentist. . . .

No matter that the lordly Black woman saved him from ruin when the power structure to which he belonged would not, he still refused to pull her granddaughter's tooth. The author neither supports nor condemns her grandmother's traditional Christian forbearance. What she does do is illustrate alternative views of a Southern Black woman who would not be subjugated by such unconscionable oppression—essential visions of a "composite self." . . .

The Trauma of a Child's Rape

Unlike her poetry, which is a continuation of traditional oral expression in Afro-American literature, Angelou's prose follows classic technique in nonpoetic Western forms. The material in each book while chronologically marking her life is nonetheless arranged in loosely structured plot sequences which are skillfully controlled. In *Caged Bird* the tenuous psyche of a gangly, sensitive, withdrawn child is traumatically jarred by rape, a treacherous act from which neither the reader nor the protagonist has recovered by the book's end. All else is cathartic: her uncles' justified revenge upon the rapist, her years of readjustment in a closed world of speechlessness despite the warm nurturing of her grandmother, her granduncle, her beloved brother Bailey, and the Stamps community; a second reunion with her vivacious mother; even her absurdly unlucky pregnancy at the end does not assuage the reader's anticipatory wonder: isn't the act of rape by a trusted adult so assaultive upon an eight-year-old's life that it leaves a wound which can never be healed? Such reader interest in a character's future is the craft from which quality fiction is made. Few autobiographers however have the verve to seize the drama of such moment, using one specific incident to control the book but with underlining implication that the incident will not control a life. . . .

Self-Construction

The four-volume autobiography effectively banishes several stereotypical myths about Black women which had remained unanswered in national literature. Angelou casts a new mold of Mother Earth—a Black woman who repositions herself in the universe so that she chooses the primary objects of her service. And ultimately that object may even be herself. Self-reconstruction of the "I" is a demanding, complex literary mode which not only exercises tested rudiments of fiction but also departs from the more accepted form of biography. Just as in fiction, the biographer can imagine or improvise a character's motives; but the autobiographer is the one narrator who really knows the truth—as well, that is, as any of us can truly know ourselves. In divulging that truth Angelou reveals a new totality of archetypal Black woman: a composite self that corrects omissions in national history and provides seldom-seen role models for cultural criteria.

Showing One's Human Side

Pierre A. Walker

Pierre A. Walker, professor at Salem State College, is editor of
The Complete Letters of Henry James *(2006) and* James on
Culture *(1995).*

When they were slaves, African Americans were considered prop-
erty, not really human beings. Ever since, slave narratives and
other African American autobiographies not only unveil social
evils, but strive to establish African Americans as human beings.
As Pierre A. Walker argues, many African Americans felt the best
way to show their human status was to become accomplished
writers of "high art," an achievement considered to be of the
highest orders of human civilization.

Many African-American texts were written to create a particular political impact. As a result, one can hardly ignore either the political conditions in which the slave narratives and [author] Richard Wright's early works, for example,
were composed or the political impact their authors (and editors and publishers, at least of the slave narratives) intended
them to have. Even African-American texts that are not obviously part of a protest tradition are received in a political context, as is clear from the tendency in much critical commen-
tary on [author] Zora Neale Hurston to demonstrate an elusive
element of protest in her novels.

So important is the political to the experience of African-
American literature that it comes as no surprise that the in-
creasing incorporation of the African-American literary tradition into mainstream academic literary studies since 1980
coincides exactly with the increasingly greater significance of

the political in the prevailing critical paradigm: what better for a political literary criticism to address than an overtly political literature?

The problem is that African-American literature has, on more than one occasion, relied on confirming its status as literature to accomplish its political aims. Since slavery relied on a belief that those enslaved were not really human beings, slave narrators responded by writing books that emphasized the fact that they themselves were humans who deserved to be treated as such. Since emancipation, African-American authors have used the same strategy to fight the belief in racial hierarchies that relegated them to second-class citizen status. One way to do this was to produce "high art," which was supposed to be one of the achievements of the highest orders of human civilization. African-American poetry provides many examples of this strategy: Claude McKay's and Countee Cullen's reliance on traditional, European poetic forms and James Weldon Johnson's "O Black and Unknown Bards." Cullen's "Yet Do I Marvel," for instance, relies on recognizable English "literary" features: Shakespearean sonnet form, rhyme, meter, references to Greek mythology, and the posing of a theological question as old as the Book of Job and as familiar as William Blake's "The Tyger."

Literary Dismissal of Racial Autobiography

Thus for a critical style to dismiss the closely related categories of form and of literature is to relegate to obscurity an important tradition of African-American literature and an important political tool of the struggle in the United States of Americans of African descent. This is clearly true in respect to *Caged Bird*, which displays the kind of literary unity that would please [critic Cleanth] Brooks, but to the significant political end of demonstrating how to fight racism. Angelou wrote *Caged Bird* in the late 1960s at the height of the New Criticism, and therefore in order for it to be the *literary* autobiography . . . , Angelou's book had to display features considered at the time typical of literature, such as organic unity. This is a political gesture, since in creating a text that satisfies contemporary criteria of "high art," Angelou underscores one of the book's central themes: how undeservedly its protagonist was relegated to second-class citizenship in her early years. To ignore form in discussing Angelou's book, therefore, would mean ignoring a critical dimension of its important political work.

Because scholarly discussions of Angelou's autobiographical works have only appeared in any significant number in the last fifteen years, *Caged Bird* and her other books have avoided—or, depending on one's view, been spared—the kind of formal analysis typically associated with New Criticism or Structuralism Scholarly critics of *Caged Bird*, often influenced by feminist and African-American studies, have focused on such issues as whether the story of Angelou's young protagonist is personal or universal, or on race, gender, identity, displacement, or a combination of these. In relation to these issues, they discuss important episodes like the scene with the "powhitetrash" girls; young Maya's rape and subsequent muteness, her experience with Mrs. Flowers, the graduation, the visit to the dentist, Maya's month living in a junkyard, or her struggle to become a San Francisco streetcar conductor. What they do not do is analyze these episodes as Angelou constructed them—often juxtaposing disparate incidents within an episode—and arranged and organized them, often undermining the chronology of her childhood story and juxtaposing the events of one chapter with the events of preceding and following ones so that they too comment on each other. The critics do not explore how Angelou, who has never denied the principle of selection in the writing of autobiography shaped the material of her childhood and adolescent life story in *Caged Bird* to present Maya's first sixteen years, much as a *bildungsroman* [novel about the moral and psychological growth of the main character] would, as a progressive process of affirming identity, learning about words, and resisting racism. What scholars have focused on in *Caged Bird* does merit attention, but an attention to the formal strategies Angelou uses to emphasize what the book expresses about identity and race reveals a sequence of lessons about resisting racist oppression, a sequence that leads Maya progressively from helpless rage and indignation to forms of subtle resistance and finally to outright and active protest. . . .

Responding to White Oppression

Because chapters eighteen and nineteen [of *Caged Bird*] explore the limits to subtle but passive resistance, the book has to go on to present other possible ways of responding to white oppression. The climactic response, one that consists of active resistance and outright protest, is Maya's persisting and breaking the color line of the San Francisco streetcar company, described in the thirty-fourth chapter. Since *Caged Bird* was written in the late sixties, at the height of the black power movement and at a time that was still debating the value of Martin Luther King's belief in nonviolent protest, it is no surprise that this act of protest is the climactic moment of resistance to white oppression in the book, a moment that says: Momma's type of resistance was fine in its time and place, but now it is time for some real action. There are at least, three other episodes in the second half of *Caged Bird*, however, that explore the line between subtle but passive resistance and active, open protest: the graduation scene (chapter twenty-three), the dentist scene (chapter twenty-four), and the story Daddy Clidell's friend, Red Leg, tells about double-crossing a white con man (chapter twenty-nine).

Falling as they do between the Joe Louis chapter and the San Francisco streetcar company chapter, these . . . episodes chart the transition from subtle resistance to active protest. The graduation scene for the most part follows the early, entirely positive examples of subtle resistance in *Caged Bird*. The only difference is that the resistance is no longer so subtle and that it specifically takes the form of poetry, which in itself valorizes the African-American literary tradition as a source for resisting white racist oppression. Otherwise, the graduation chapter conforms to the pattern established by the "powhitetrash" and Mrs. Cullinan chapters: first, there is the insult by the white person, when the speaker tells the black audience about all the improvements that the white school will receive—improvements that far surpass the few scheduled for the black school. There is Maya's first response of humiliation and anger: "Then I wished that Gabriel Prosser and Nat Turner had killed all whitefolks in their bed." shared now by the community: "[T]he proud graduating class of 1940 had dropped their head." Then there is the action on the part of a member of the black community—Henry Reed's improvised leading the audience in "Lift Ev'ry Voice and Sing"—that at the same time avoids an irreversible confrontation with the white oppressor and permits the black community to feel its dignity and superiority: "We were on top again. As always, again. We survive." . . .

Within strictly legal confines, such an ability is the essence of the American myth of success, and undoubtedly, at least part of the appeal of *Caged Bird* is that it corresponds both to this definition of black heroism and to the outline of a typical success story. The product of a broken family, raped at age eight, Angelou was offered at first "only the crumbs" from her "country's table." She suffers from an inferiority complex, an identity crisis, and the humiliation of racist insults. By the end of the book, however, she no longer feels inferior, knows who she is, and knows that she can respond to racism in ways that preserve her dignity and her life, liberty, and property, and she knows—and demonstrates in addition through the very, existence of the book itself—that she can respond by using the power of words. It may be impossible to convince a poststructuralist that there is something uniquely literary about Angelou's autobiography, but certainly part of what this autobiography is about is the power and utility of literature and its own genesis and existence as a protest against racism.

Principle or Compromise in Race Relations

Mary Jane Lupton

Mary Jane Lupton, a retired professor at Morgan State University, is a prolific writer whose books include Lucille Clifton: Her Life and Letters (2006) *and* James Welch: A Critical Companion *(2004).*

I Know Why the Caged Bird Sings *portrays a conflict between Angelou and her grandmother over how to deal with racism. Angelou sees her grandmother as strong, smart, and "ten feet tall with eight-foot arms," but doesn't understand why she won't directly confront white people.*

What distinguishes [Maya] Angelou's autobiographical method from more conventional autobiographical forms is her very denial of closure. The reader of autobiography expects a beginning, a middle, and an end—as occurs in [*I Know Why the Caged Bird Sings*]. She or he also expects a central experience, as we indeed are given in the extraordinary rape sequence of *Caged Bird*. But Angelou, by continuing her narrative, denies the form and its history, creating from each ending a new beginning, relocating the center to some luminous place in a volume yet to be. Stretching the autobiographical canvas, she moves forward [in *Caged Bird*]: from being a child; to being a mother. . . .

Birthing Another Book

The "sense of life begetting life" at the end of *Caged Bird* can no longer signal the conclusion of the narrative. The autobiographical moment has been reopened and expanded; [her

Mary Jane Lupton, "Singing the Black Mother: Maya Angelou and Autobiographical Continuity," *Black American Literature Forum*, vol. 24, no. 2, summer 1990, pp. 257–276. Copyright © 1990 Mary Jane Lupton. Reproduced by permission of the author.

son's] birth can now be seen symbolically as the birth of another text. In a 1975 interview with Carol Benson, Angelou uses such a birthing metaphor in describing the writing of [her next autobiography, published in 1974] *Gather Together [in My Name]*. "If you have a child, it takes nine months. It took me three-and-a-half years to write *Gather Together*, so I couldn't just drop it." This statement makes emphatic what in the autobiographies are much more elusive comparisons between creative work and motherhood; after a three-and-a-half-year pregnancy she gives birth to *Gather Together*, indicating that she must have planned the conception of the second volume shortly after the 1970 delivery of *Caged Bird*.

The Working Black Woman

["Momma"] Annie [Angelou's grandmother] Henderson is a solid, God-fearing, economically independent woman whose general store in Stamps, Arkansas, is the "lay center activities in town," much as Annie is the moral center of the family. According to Mildred A. Hill-Lubin, the grandmother, both in Africa and in America, "has been a significant force in the stability and the continuity of the Black family and the community." Hill-Lubin selects Annie Henderson as her primary example of the strong grandmother in African-American literature—the traditional preserver of the family, the source of folk wisdom, and the instiller of values within the Black community. Throughout *Caged Bird* Maya has ambivalent feelings for this awesome woman, whose values of self-determination and personal dignity gradually chip away at Maya's dreadful sense of being "shit color." As a self-made woman, Annie Henderson has the economic power to lend money to whites; as a practical Black woman, however, she is convinced that whites cannot be directly confronted: "If she had been asked and had chosen to answer the question of whether she was cowardly or not, she would have said that she was a realist." To survive in a racist society, Momma Henderson has had to develop a realistic strategy of submission that Maya finds unacceptable. Maya, in her need to re-image her grandmother, creates a metaphor that places Momma's power above any apparent submissiveness: Momma "did an excellent job of sagging from her waist down, but from the waist up she seemed to be pulling for the top of the oak tree across the road."

There are numerous episodes, both in *Caged Bird* and *Gather Together*, which involve the conflict between Maya and her grandmother over how to deal with racism. When taunted by three "powhitetrash" girls, Momma quietly sings a hymn; Maya, enraged, would like to have a rifle. Or, when humiliated by a white dentist who'd rather put his "hand in a dog's mouth than in a nigger's," Annie is passive; Maya subsequently invents a fantasy in which Momma runs the dentist out of town. In the italicized dream text, Maya endows her grandmother with superhuman powers; Momma magically changes the dentist's nurse into a bag of chicken seed. In reality the grandmother has been defeated and humiliated, her only reward a mere ten dollars in interest for a loan she had made to the dentist. In Maya's fantasy Momma's "eyes were blazing like live coals and her arms had doubled themselves in length"; in actuality she "looked tired."

This richly textured passage is rendered from the perspective of an imaginative child who re-creates her grandmother— but in a language that ironically transforms Annie Henderson from a Southern Black storekeeper into an eloquent heroine from a romantic novel: "Her tongue had thinned and the words rolled off well enunciated." Instead of the silent "nigra" of the actual experience, Momma Henderson is now the articulate defender of her granddaughter against the stuttering dentist. Momma Henderson orders the "contemptuous scoundrel" to leave Stamps "now and herewith." The narrator eventually lets Momma speak normally, then comments: "(She could afford to slip into the vernacular because she had such eloquent command of English.)"

In a sign of the gradual turn of public opinion against racism and segregation, a 1943 mass meeting is held in Chicago to discuss ways to fight both Nazi Germany and the South's Jim Crow system of oppression. Gordon Coster/Time & Life Pictures/Getty Images.

This fantasy is the narrator's way of dealing with her ambivalence towards Momma Henderson—a woman who throughout *Caged Bird* represents to Maya both strength and weakness, both generosity and punishment, both affection and the denial of affection. Here her defender is "ten feet tall with eight-foot arms," quite capable, to recall the former tree image, of reaching the top of an oak from across the road. Momma's physical transformation in the dream text also recalls an earlier description: "I saw only her power and strength. She was taller than any woman in my personal world, and her hands were so large they could span my head from ear to ear." In the dentist fantasy, Maya eliminates all of Momma Henderson's "negative" traits—submissiveness, severity, religiosity, sternness, down-home speech. It would seem that Maya is so shattered by her grandmother's reaction to Dentist Lincoln, so destroyed by her illusions of Annie Henderson's power in relationship to white people, that she compensates by reversing the true situation and having the salivating dentist be the target of Momma's wrath. Significantly, this transformation occurs immediately before Momma Henderson tells Maya and Bailey that they are going to California. Its position in the text gives it the impression of finality. Any negative attitudes become submerged, only to surface later, in *Gather Together*, as aspects of Angelou's own ambiguity towards race, power, and identity.

Momma as Security and Punishment

In *Caged Bird* Momma Henderson had hit Maya with a switch for unknowingly taking the Lord's name in vain, "like whitefolks do." Similarly, in *Gather Together* Annie slaps her granddaughter after Maya, on a visit to Stamps, verbally assaults two white saleswomen. In a clash with Momma Henderson that is both painful and final, Maya argues for "the principle of the thing," and Momma slaps her. Surely, Momma's slap is well intended; she wishes to protect Maya from "lunatic cracker boys" and men in white sheets, from all of the insanity of racial prejudice. The "new" Maya, who has been to the city and found a sense of independence, is caught in the clash between her recently acquired "principles" and Momma's fixed ideology. Thus the slap—but also the intention behind it—will remain in Maya's memory long after the mature Angelou has been separated from Annie Henderson's supervision. Momma makes Maya and the baby leave Stamps, again as a precaution: "Momma's intent to protect me had caused her to hit me in the face, a thing she had never done, and to send me away to where she thought I'd be safe." Maya departs on the train, never to see her grandmother again.

Silenced No More

Sandi Russell

Sandi Russell, a Harlem native, is a jazz singer and a writer. She is author of the novel Tidewater *and coeditor of* Virgo Book of Love Poetry.

After the Civil War, little changed for black women. Many remained in their stations as domestics and field hands, kept there largely by segregation and threats of violence. When autobiographies of African American writers first appeared, the silence about racial grievances was broken.

Author Sandi Russell contends that Maya Angelou and other African American women are in a dilemma. They need the traditions of the past to affirm their selfhood; yet they also need to shed those traditions to assert their independence and pride.

The Great Migration lured millions of blacks away from the soil of sorrow, to Northern and Midwestern America. Some remained in the small towns of the South that were nearly decimated by this mass movement. And often, it was a very difficult decision. . . .

Of those who did remain, almost all tried to form a tight and cohesive community that would enable them to endure the "slave" work sharecropping, Jim Crow laws, no voting rights, the Ku Klux Klan, rampant racism and persistent poverty.

Black women, working in fields or in some white woman's home, tried to keep up their spiritual strength to see them through. Some were able to persevere; others, beset by racism, saw themselves and their families demolished by it. Yet most managed to keep alive the sustaining rituals that were the ba-

Sandi Russell, from *African American Women Writers from Slavery to the Present.* Copyright © 2002 by Sandi Russell. Reprinted by permission of the author.

sis of African-American life. Through song, sharing, sewing, quilting, gardening, cookery, planting, tale-telling and abundant good humour, they brought beauty to a tainted land.

These poor, black women were sustained by the richness of their culture, even if the larger world dismissed its existence. The only times they heard their voices ring out were in church, across a field or yard, in someone's kitchen or, quite often, in a small private place in their minds.

Through the literature of Alice Walker and the autobiographies of Maya Angelou, a voice has been given to that "small place", and those silenced women have been allowed to speak. Complex, contrary, battered and brave, the lives of those black Southern women instruct and inform us; but above all, they inspire. . . .

Angelou's Silence and Songs

Maya Angelou is indeed phenomenal. Poet, singer, dancer, composer, actress, director, editor and autobiographer, her "reach" embraces both writing and the performing arts. As a black autobiographer, Ms. Angelou stands beside the escaped slave Frederick Douglass. Like him, she can win the minds of her audience and speak not only for herself, but for her race. She admits to taking on this representative role in the first volume of her autobiography [*I Know Why the Caged Bird Sings*]. . . .

The five volumes of Maya Angelou's life story span almost half a century, from the late 1920s to the early 1970s. They resonate with the love, wit, energy and spirit of an indomitable woman. Maya was initially reluctant to write about her life, but her editor, Robert Loomis, ensnared her by saying: "To write an autobiography as literature, is the most difficult thing anyone could do." That was all the challenge Maya needed.

Yet, to take up such a challenge and succeed, the black woman needs all her ancestral powers of survival. . . .

The church, with its moments of spirited singing and abandoned shouting, egged on by a masterful preacher, studded [Angelou's] Sundays [when she was a child].

This nurturing world was to crumble when Maya was eight years old. She went to visit her mother in St. Louis and the unimaginable happened. Maya Angelou was raped by her mother's boyfriend. The mere fact that Maya, having been abandoned by her mother, returned to her only to be raped by a man her mother saw fit to have a relationship with, must have devastated this eight-year-old child beyond comprehension. This horror was compounded by the "silencing" of the event and the killing of the rapist by her uncles. Maya's last, small semblance of selfhood collapsed. She sealed herself up. . . .

Maya remained silent for five years. We wonder what painful and confused ragings must have gone on in her young head. But Maya's resolve, turned inward in those years, allows us to understand the woman she was to become. When that tenacity and strength of purpose were eventually turned outward, they enabled her to confront and overcome the many obstacles that life was to offer her. The individual who was able to bring Maya out of her silenced world was Mrs. Flowers, the gentle, caring "black aristocrat" of Stamps. She read literature and recited poetry with such grace and beauty that Maya herself was moved to do the same. Ms. Angelou stated that Mrs. Flowers "made me proud to be a Negro, just by being herself."

Moving from the small world of Stamps to the big-city life of San Francisco, Maya began her determined struggle to make a place for herself in the world.

In this moving and brilliantly written first volume, we learn what people and forces came to mould Maya Angelou. And it is Maya, the author, who goes through and to her life as the child Marguerite, and recounts it with extraordinary skill and insight.

There are few autobiographies that read with such depth and articulation. We must stop and remind ourselves that yes, this is a life, not a fiction. And it is Maya's life of strength, love, and determination that we can use as a mirror to judge our own....

The White's Stereotype

All God's Children Need Traveling Shoes (1986) is Maya Angelou's fifth autobiographical volume. It concerns itself with the problematic idea that African Americans can claim Africa as their homeland. Proud and liberated Ghana, with President [Kwame] Nkrumah at its head, does not yet know its African-American cousins. The white world's stereotypic image of black Americans still predominates in this country. Ms. Angelou is left to consider her position there....

Struggling to find her place in this "homeland," Ms. Angelou's writing conveys the questions that plague her, and which she is never able fully to answer: "Was the odor of slavery so obvious that people were offended and lashed out at us automatically?" ... Throughout this volume, Maya Angelou can never really come to terms with this painful cultural divide, and never really manages to confront its deeper issues. Perhaps the situation was too overwhelming and still too close to address in a more probing manner:

> If the heart of Africa still remained elusive, my search for it had brought me closer to understanding myself and other human beings.

Ms. Angelou comes to understand that she is indeed an American, and that, for better or for worse, that land is her home:

> Many of us had only begun to realize in Africa that the Stars and Stripes was our flag and our only flag, and that knowledge was almost too painful to bear ...

> I shuddered to think that while we wanted that flag dragged into the mud and sullied beyond repair, we also wanted it

pristine ... Watching it wave in the breeze of a distance made us nearly choke with emotion. It lifted us up with its promise and broke our hearts with its denial.

A Black Girl's Continuing Death and Rebirth

Liliane K. Arensberg

Liliane K. Arensberg is on the faculty of Marshall University.

Author Liliane K. Arensberg stresses the devastating effects that displacement and abandonment have on African American children. The young Marguerite experiences both. Two things save her: a flexibility that allows her to adapt as she moves from place to place and her dependence on one solid constant in her life—books.

In spite of her adaptability and books, Marguerite suffers intense pain from her abandonment, coming to believe that she is really an orphan, unwanted by anyone because she is homely and black. Her anguish is worsened when she is raped, after which she refuses to speak for five years.

"What you looking at me for? I didn't come to stay. . . ."

Indeed, geographic movement and temporary residence become formative aspects of [Maya Angelou's] growing identity—equal in importance to experiences and relationships more commonly regarded as instrumental in forming the adult self. Appropriately, this poetic phrase [from the introduction of *I Know Why the Caged Bird Sings*] becomes the young girl's motto or "shield" as Angelou calls it; Maya's means of proclaiming her isolation while defending against its infringement.

Shuttled between temporary homes and transient allegiances, Maya necessarily develops a stoic flexibility that be-

Liliane K. Arensberg, "Death as Metaphor of Self in *I Know Why the Caged Bird Sings*," *CLA Journal*, vol. 20, December 1976, pp. 275–291. Copyright © 1976 by The College Language Association. Used by permission of The College Language Association.

comes not only her "shield," but, more importantly, her characteristic means of dealing with the world. This flexibility is both blessing and curse: it enables her to adapt to various and changing environments, but it also keeps her forever threatened with loss or breakdown of her identity. . .

Indeed, Angelou's descriptions of her younger self seem almost entirely comprised of negatives: she is not wanted by her parents who hold over her the unspoken, but everpresent, threat of banishment; she is not beautiful or articulate like her brother, Bailey; she is too introverted and passive to assert herself on her environment; and, finally, she is a child in a world of enigmatic adults, and a black girl in a world created by and for the benefit of white men.

Furthermore, Maya's geographic worlds are each separate and self-contained. There is the world of Momma and her Store in Stamps, a puritan world of racial pride, religious devotion and acquiescence to one's worldly lot. And there is her "wild and beautiful" mother's world of pool halls, card sharks, fast dancing, fast talking and fast loving. Combining and transcending both is the private and portable world of Maya's imagination.

If there is one stable element in Angelou's youth it is this dependence on books. . . .

Self-Hate and Abandonment

Angelou's highly personal confession of racial self-hatred is, unfortunately, not unique in Afro-American experience. Many works of contemporary black novelists and autobiographers—from Ralph Ellison and Imamu Baraka/LeRoi Jones to Richard Wright and Malcolm X—assert that invisibility, violence, alienation and death are part and parcel of growing up black in a white America. Likewise, psychological and sociological studies affirm that the first lesson in living taught the black child is how to ensure his/her survival. "The child must know," write [William] Grier and [Price] Cobbs, "that the white world is dangerous and that if he does not understand its rules it may kill him." It is, then, pitifully understandable for Maya to wish herself white, since blackness forebodes annihilation.

Of equal significance, in this introductory anecdote is Maya's belief that a stepmother has put her under this spell and then abandoned her. Her image of herself, for at least the first five years of life, is that of an orphan. Even later, when forced to recognize the existence of both her parents, she still clings to this orphan identity. Although acknowledging that Bailey, by dint of beauty and personality, is his parents' true son, she describes herself as "an orphan that they had picked up to provide Bailey with company."

While her father is as culpable as her mother in Maya's abandonment, it is nevertheless her mother whom Maya most yearns for and consequently blames. No real mother would "laugh and eat oranges in the sunshine without her children," Maya reflects bitterly when first confronted with her mother's existence. No proper mother should let her child so profoundly mourn her passing as Maya has done. . . .

Death and Race

Upon her return to Stamps, Maya projects her own death-like inertness on the whole town. It is described as "exactly what I wanted, without will or consciousnes. . . . Entering Stamps, I had the feeling that I was stepping over the border lines of the map and would fall, without fear, right off the end of the world. Nothing more could happen, for in Stamps nothing happened."

An outcast in a community of outcasts, Maya avoids emotional ties with others. In fact, for six years, until Louise befriends her, Maya is without an intimate friend her own age. It is not surprising, then, that when Mrs. Bertha Flowers takes an active interest in her, Maya describes her as "the lady who threw me my first life line." Nor is it surprising that Maya turns to the safety of books for the exciting relationships shunned in real life. . . .

Death in its many manifestations is, indeed, pivotal to Maya Angelou's sense of self. In fact, the tension between Maya's quest for a positive, life-affirming identity and her obsession with annihilation provide the unconscious dynamism affecting all aspects of her narrative, and endowing it with power and conviction. Thus, the ultimate challenge to death is Maya's own active assertion of self and her willingness to face annihilation and overcome it. The remainder of Angelou's autobiography addresses itself to this end.

The Journey Inward

Dolly A. McPherson

Dolly A. McPherson is retired from the faculty at Wake Forest University in Winston-Salem, North Carolina, but still serves as literary executor of the Maya Angelou Archives at Wake Forest.

Maya Angelou's I Know Why the Caged Bird Sings *is different from other African American stories of the South because the essence of the work is the spiritual aspect of survival, the innermost reaction to surroundings and events. Angelou's emphasis is on the psychological impact of her grandmother, the community, and the church. The African American community in Stamps, Arkansas is a place where neighbors help one another and where community rites and traditions lift the spirit. As Marguerite grows up, community becomes redefined, enlarged but less supportive and personal.*

I *Know Why the Caged Bird Sings* (hereafter called *Caged Bird*) is a carefully conceived record of a young girl's slow and clumsy growth. It is also a record of her initiation into her world and her discovery of her interior identity. In *Caged Bird*, Angelou first confidently reaches back in memory to pull out the painful times: when she and her brother Bailey fail to understand the adult code and, therefore, break laws they know nothing of; when they swing easily from hysterical laughter to desperate loneliness, from a hunger for heroes to the voluntary pleasure-pain game of wondering who their *real* parents are and how long it will be before they come to take them to their *real* home. Growing up in Stamps, Arkansas, as Maya Angelou describes those long-ago years, is a continual struggle against surrender to the very large adults, who, being

Dolly A. McPherson, from *Order Out of Chaos: The Autobiographical Works of Maya Angelou.* New York: Peter Lang, 1990. Copyright © 1990 Peter Lang Publishing, Inc., New York. All rights reserved. Reproduced by permission.

Black, practiced and taught special traditions whose roots were buried in Africa or had been created during centuries of slavery. According to these traditions, a good child dropped her eyes when speaking to an adult; a good child spoke softly; a good child never resisted the idea that Whites were better, cleaner, or more intelligent than Blacks. Growing up and surviving as a young girl in the South of the 1930s and early 1940s is a painful experience for a young girl whose world is colored by disillusion and despair, aloneness, self-doubt, and a diminished sense of self.

Indeed, Angelou underscores her diminished sense of self and the rootlessness of her early childhood years when she proclaims in the prologue:

> What are you looking at me for? I didn't come to stay . . .

The words are painfully appropriate, for the young Maya then Marguerite Johnson, is a shy, tensely self-conscious child who believes that her true beauty is obscured. As she struggles to remember her lines, she is conscious of her dual self, which is the constant subject of her fantasies. Beneath the ugly disguise—a lavender taffeta dress remade from a White woman's discard, broad feet, and gap-teeth—is the real Marguerite.

Such fantasies are ephemeral and the time comes when the young girl must face the painful reality of her being. . . .

Caught in a Black Dream

For Maya there is no magical metamorphosis, no respite from her "black dream." On this Easter Sunday, she understands the futility of her wish to become "one of the sweet little white girls who were everybody's dream of what is right with the world." Unlike Christ, whose resurrection from death the church is commemorating, Maya cannot be reborn into another life where she will be White and perfect and wonderful. Pained by this reality and by the impossibility of her White fantasy, Maya flees from the church "peeing and crying" her way home.

This scene re-creates graphically the dynamics of many young Black girls' disillusionment and imprisonment in American society. . . .

The young Maya not only lives in a society which defines beauty in White terms of physical beauty, but she also internalizes these notions. In a letter (February 4, 1966) to her long-time friend Rosa Guy, Angelou wrote, "My belief [as a child] that I was ugly was absolute, and nobody tried to disabuse me—not even Momma. Momma's love enfolded me like an umbrella but at no time did she try to dissuade me of my belief that I was an ugly child."

In this letter and in the autobiography as well, Angelou offers important insights into the effects of social conditioning on the mind and emotions of a Black child growing up in a hostile environment. Writing from the perspective of adulthood, the older Angelou reveals that, within this imprisoning environment, there is no place for the young Maya; that she is a displaced person whose pain is intensified by her awareness of her displacement. . . .

Whiteness to the Child

White dominance intrudes on other occasions that also teach Maya vital lessons in courage and survival and open her eyes to the fact that she belongs to an oppressed class. In Uncle Willie, for example, she sees the dual peril of being Black and crippled when he is forced to hide in the potato bin when the sheriff casually warns Grandmother Henderson that local White lynchers will be on a rampage in the Black community. Through this terrifying experience, Maya learns that lameness offers no protection from the wrath of bigots.

Other occasions provide proof of a predatory White world and of White ritualistic violence against the Black male, for example, when Bailey sees the castrated body of a Black man. Horrified by what he has seen but not understood, Bailey begins to ask questions that are dangerous for a young Black boy in the Arkansas of 1940. The incident leads Angelou to conclude bitterly that "the Black woman in the South who raises sons, grandsons and nephews had her heartstrings tied to a hanging noose." Years later, when Angelou must fight for the opportunity to become the first Black person hired as a conductor on the San Francisco streetcar, she learns that White racism is not merely a problem of the South but an evil that penetrates most aspects of American life.

While intrusion from the outside world provides experiences that increase the child's awareness of her social displacement, the Store, where Blacks congregate before and after work, teaches Maya the meaning of economic discrimination. By keenly observing the cotton workers who visit the Store, she gains insight into their inner lives. In the early dawn hours, Maya observes the cotton workers, gay and full of morning vigor, as they wait for the wagons to come and take them to the fields. Optimistic that the harvest will be good and not choosing to recall the disappointments of the recent past, the workers josh each other and flaunt their readiness to pick two or three hundred pounds of cotton this day. Even the children promise "to bring home fo' bits." The later afternoons, however, reveal the actual harshness of Black Southern life. In the receding sunlight, "the people [drag themselves], rather than their empty sacks." . . .

Conflicting Communities

For Maya, Stamps and St. Louis stand in sharp contrast. In Stamps, there are Grandmother Henderson and the Store; there are also religious devotion and the acceptance of one's worldly and racial lot. In the closely knit rural community, Maya knows all the Black people in town, and they know her. For the young Maya, Stamps is a symbol of order; in fact, the orderliness of the store—the carefully arranged shelves, the counters, and the cutting boards—reflects the orderliness of her life in general. In St. Louis, however, Angelou is thrown into her mother's world of taverns, pool halls, gambling, fast living and fast loving. This is a far looser environment than Maya had ever known and one that is devoid of the customary laws that Grandmother Henderson had taught her to respect. The range of sanctioned behavior is also broader, individuals are less stringently controlled by moral laws or social pressures, and relations among individuals are less stable. Although Maya lives comfortably in St. Louis and is excited by many aspects of urban life, she remains a stranger among strangers, mainly because the urban community treats the individual as individual rather than as part of a group, and so is powerless to provide her the emotional security she needs. Moreover, having spent four years in the solitude of Stamps, Maya is dislocated by the strangeness of her new environment: the tremendous noise of the city, its "scurrying sounds," its frightening claustrophobia. Grandmother Baxter's German accent and elegant manners are also unfamiliar. Her mother, aunts and uncles are equally unreal. St. Louis provides Maya neither sense of place nor permanence. Indeed, after only a few weeks there, she understands that it is not her real home. . . .

Throughout her recaptured childhood years in Stamps, Angelou examines herself introspectively. Though, Angelou, the autobiographer, locates herself in the physical environment of her childhood—in a series of physical scenes—her inward retrospective musings and the interiority that she manages to capture so well are more significant to the reader's understanding of the autobiographer's private self than of the external phenomena from which the musing emerge.

Maya lives in "perfect personal silence" for nearly five years until she meets Mrs. Bertha Flowers, Stamps' Black intellectual, who will become for the adult Angelou her "measure of what a human being can be." Mrs. Flowers throws Maya her "first life line" by accepting her as an individual, not in relation to another person. Moreover, Mrs. Flowers ministers to

Racial tensions could lead to violence in the North as well as the South. Here a mob of angry whites is being dispersed by tear gas during a 1943 race riot in Detroit, Michigan. AP Images.

Maya's growing hunger and quest for individuality by giving her books of poetry, talking to her philosophically about books, and encouraging her to recite poems. Committing poems to memory, pondering them, recalling them when lonely, give Maya a sense of power within herself, a transcendence over her immediate environment.

Maya's "lessons in living" with Mrs. Flowers awaken her conscience, sharpen her perspective of her environment and of the relationship between Blacks and the larger society, and teach her something about the beauty and power of language. Emotionally and intellectually strengthened by this friendship, Maya begins to compose poetic verses and ring songs, and to keep a scrapbook journal in which she records her reactions to and impressions of people, places and events, and new ideas that she is introduced to by books. . . .

Maya Strikes Back

As Angelou chronicles her movements from innocence to awareness, from childhood to adolescence, there are certain social barriers that she must confront and overcome in order to maintain a sense of self and relative freedom.

For example, Angelou's first confrontation with a White person catapults her into a clearer awareness of social reality and into a growing consciousness of self-worth. This confrontation proves to be a major turning point in her life. During a brief time when she was eleven years old, Maya worked in the home of Mrs. Viola Cullinan, a wealthy, transplanted Virginian. With the arrogance of a Southern White woman whom neither custom nor tradition had taught to respect a Black person, Mrs. Cullinan insults Maya by calling her Mary rather than Marguerite, a name that Mrs. Cullinan considered too cumbersome. Mrs. Cullinan's attempt to change Maya's name for her own convenience echoes the larger tradition of American racism that attempts to prescribe the nature and limitations of a Black person's identity. In refusing to address Maya by her proper name, the symbol of her individuality and uniqueness, Mrs. Cullinan refuses to acknowledge her humanity. A sensitive, reflective nature, combined with an alert intelligence, enables Maya to comprehend the nature of this insult. . . .

Maya strikes back, deliberately breaking several pieces of Mrs. Cullinan's heirloom china. In doing so, she affirms her individuality and value. Through this encounter, the young Maya learns that until the individual is willing to take a decisive step toward self-definition, refusing to compromise with insults, he or she remains in a cage. In short, the individual must resist society's effort to limit his or her aspirations. Only after Maya determines to risk Mrs. Cullinan's outrage and to defy the expectations of others is she able to begin to loose herself, psychologically, from the dehumanizing atmosphere of her environment.

Many American autobiographies besides *Cage Bird*, including *The Narrative of the Life of Frederick Douglass, Black Boy*, Maxine Hong Kingston's *Woman Warrior, The Autobiography of Malcolm X, Black Elk Speaks*, Anne Moody's *Coming of Age in Mississippi*, and others, are structured around a narrative enactment of change on two levels: the personal and psychological on one hand, and the sociohistorical and intellectual on the other. Paradoxically, while Angelou is growing in confident awareness of her strength as an individual, she is also becoming increasingly more perceptive about her identity as a member of an oppressed racial group in Stamps. In Stamps, as throughout the South, religion, sports and education functioned in ways that encouraged the discriminated class to accept the status quo. But Angelou demonstrates how Blacks in Stamps subverted those institutions and used them to withstand the cruelty of the American experience.

In a graphic description of a revival meeting, Angelou recalls her first observation of the relation between Blacks and religion. To the casual observer, the revivalists seem to "[bask] in the righteousness of the poor and the exclusiveness of the downtrodden" and to believe that "it was better to be meek and lowly, spat upon and abused for this little time" on earth. Although the poor give thanks to the Lord for a life filled with the most meager essentials and a maximum amount of brute oppression, the church rituals create for them a temporary transcendence and an articulation of spirit. However, in this tightly written, emotionally charged scene, Angelou briefly records the joining point between the blues and religious tradition. Miss Grace, the good-time woman, is also conducting rituals of transcendence through her barrelhouse blues. The agony in religion and the blues is the connecting point. . . .

Early on, the reader gleans that although the Joe Louis victories in the boxing ring in the 1930s were occasions for street celebrations that caused tens of thousands of Blacks to parade, sing, dance, and derive all the joy possible from these collective victories of the race, for Angelou, Joe Louis' victory over heavy-weight contender Primo Carnera was "a grotesque counterpoint to the normal way of life" in Arkansas. . . .

Angelou even remembers her graduation from elementary school not as the customarily exciting and happy occasion for the young graduates and their families and friends, but as a dramatization of the painful injustices of a segregated society and an underscoring of the powerlessness of Blacks within that society. As she listens to the insulting words of an oblivious and insensitive White speaker, the young girl perceives a terrifying truth about her racial self and about the desperation of impotence, especially about the impotence of Black people in the South of the 1930s. . . .

Yet, her momentarily mixed feelings of despair, shame and anger on her graduation day at the seemingly hopeless future for young Blacks in racist America are surmounted by her pride in Blacks when the Negro National Anthem is sung. As Maya consciously joins the class and audience in singing, she unconsciously, from her perspective in time, also predicts her own future as a poet. . . .

Angelou's complex awareness of what Black men, women and children encountered in their struggles for selfhood is apparent in each of these incidents. Such experiences are recorded not simply as historical events, but as symbolic revelations of Angelou's inner world. They are social, geographic and psychological occasions. The implication that one's powerlessness in the larger world may need to be experienced and overcome in the process of personal development is very clear.

In 1941, when Maya is thirteen, she and Bailey move to Oakland and later San Francisco to live with their mother whom they have not seen in six years. By this time, Vivian Baxter has married Daddy Clidell, a gambler and respected businessman, who will soon become "the first father [Maya] would know." For a while, Maya re-experiences some of the personal dislocation already felt so acutely in Stamps and St.

Louis. But in time "the air of collective displacement [and] the impermanence of life in wartime" dissipate her sense of not belonging.

Angelou and Civil Rights

Hilton Als

Hilton Als has been a staff writer for the New Yorker *since 1996.*

Book critic Hilton Als fails to give Maya Angelou's post-autobiographical career unqualified praise. He credits her with writing openly of her own experiences in the first person as the central character. And, more than most critics, he looks at the work within the national racial background against which it occurs. He underscores the great need for black women to assume leadership positions and notes that Congresswomen Shirley Chisholm and Barbara Jordan devoted themselves to such leadership. But Angelou, writes Als, did not join the political ranks with other black women writers like Toni Cade Bambara and Gayl Jones. Als claims that Angelou seems more interested in self-revelation than politics.

When *I Know Why the Caged Bird Sings* came out, in 1970, Angelou was hailed as a new kind of memoirist. As Mary Helen Washington writes in her invaluable study *Invented Lives: Narratives of Black Women 1860–1960*, black women autobiographers of the nineteenth and early twentieth centuries had been "frozen into self-consciousness by the need to defend black women and men against the vicious and prevailing stereotypes." Relegated to the margins of life, they found it difficult to rewrite themselves as central characters. Only in private could they talk about their personal lives. But Angelou took those stories public. She wrote about blackness from the inside, without apology or defense. The writer Julian Mayfield called Angelou's book "a work of art which eludes description because the black aesthetic—another way of saying 'the black experience'—has too long been neglected to be formalized by weary clichés." Angelou, Mayfield suggested, had set a precedent. . . .

Placing Angelou in the Civil Rights Struggle

The success of *I Know Why the Caged Bird Sings*, like that of many memoirs, had less to do with the originality of its writing than with its resonance in the prevailing Zeitgeist [atmosphere]. By the time *I Know Why* was published, Martin Luther King, Jr., and Malcolm X were dead, and the only hope for black politics, it seemed, lay in the voices that were just beginning to be heard: those of such strong-willed female politicians as Shirley Chisholm and Barbara Jordan, two of the first black women to serve in Congress. Chisholm and Jordan, products of the colonial West Indies and the Old South, respectively, pinned their speeches to the idea of a changing United States, and it was their brand of rhetoric—a fierce criticism of the past blended with a kind of survivor's optimism, a belief in the future of the urban family—that cleared the way for Angelou's narrative of damage, perseverance, and eventual triumph.

There is no question that *I Know Why the Caged Bird Sings* was an important contribution to the wave of black feminist writing in the seventies. . . . It has become clear that her real literary cohorts, at least in terms of affect, are not her politically minded contemporaries Toni Cade Bambara and Gayl Jones but Anaïs Nin, whose diaries, published in the late sixties and early seventies, were also heralded as feminist works, the acute renderings of a woman's soul. Nin and Angelou are both theatrical writers—they use language, often with great aplomb, to describe and glorify a self that is fulfilled only when it is being observed. Both writers, in their early books, were pioneers of self-exposure, willing to turn a spotlight on their own sometimes questionable exploits and emotional shortcomings. While Angelou and Nin tended to be more interested in self-revelation than in politics or the feminist perspective, the unabashed female personae they presented freed many other women writers to open themselves up without shame to the eyes of the world.

Over the decades, Angelou's memoirs have remained more or less consistent in structure: each volume gives a historical overview of the area where Angelou was living at the time, and of blacks against the backdrop of the local white society; then Maya emerges, her story played out within the larger context. Or is she herself the larger context? Angelou's original goal—to tell the truth about the lives of black women—seems, after her first volume, to have evolved into something else: to document the ups and downs of her own life. The critic Selwyn Cudjoe writes of *Gather Together*, "Angelou is still concerned with the questions of what it means to be black and female in America and exactly where she fits into the scheme of things. But her development is reflective of a particular type of black woman, located at a particular moment of history. . . . It is almost as though the incidents in the text were simply gathered together under the name of Maya Angelou but not so organized to achieve that complex level of signification that one expects in such a work." . . .

In the latest installment, *A Song Flung Up to Heaven*, we see Angelou returning from Africa, in 1964, at the invitation of Malcolm X. He had a mission for her—or did he? It is never quite clear whether he asked her to join him or she offered herself up. "Malcolm X, on his last visit to Accra, had announced a desire to create a foundation he called the Organization of African-American Unity," she explains. "The idea was so stimulating to the community of African-American residents that I persuaded myself I should return to the States to help establish the organization. . . . When I informed [others] that I had started making plans to go back to America to work with Malcolm, they—my friends, buddies, pals—began to treat me as if I had suddenly become special. . . . My stature had definitely increased." When she arrives in the States, however, Angelou postpones her meeting with Malcolm X for a month. He is assassinated two days later, and Maya returns to her night-club act. Eventually, she becomes a market researcher in the Watts district of Los Angeles, where her work is interrupted by the 1965 riots. (On her third day of avoiding the riots, Angelou recalls her mother's saying, "Nothing's wrong with going to jail for something you believe in," and decides to return to Watts, "ready to be arrested," but no policemen take the bait.) At the end of the book, Martin Luther King asks Angelou to take a trip around the country to promote the S.C.L.C. [Southern Christian Leadership Conference]. She agrees somewhat reluctantly, but again postpones—this time in order to throw herself a birthday party. Five weeks later, on her birthday, King is assassinated. . . .

The publication, in the nineties, of what can best be described as Angelou's wisdom books—*Wouldn't Take Nothing for My Journey Now* and *Even the Stars Look Lonesome*—seems a more natural culmination of her work. Collections of homilies strung together with autobiographical texts, they stress the all-important "inner" journey. "The woman who survives intact and happy must be at once tender and tough," Angelou writes in *Wouldn't Take Nothing*. "She must have convinced herself, or be in the unending process of convincing herself, that she, her values, and her choices are important." Angelou's memoirs are ample evidence that she has convinced herself of this. Her readers are another matter.

Social Issues in Literature

CHAPTER 3

Contemporary Perspectives on Racism

The Changing Face of Racial Conflict

Roberto Lovato

Roberto Lovato is a writer with New America Media and is a frequent contributor to The Nation. *One of his books is* The Micropolitics of Immigration.

The racial profile of inner cities has changed radically since the 1950s. Many in law enforcement believe that a new racial war has developed—one between African Americans and Latinos, partially over the competition for jobs. The gangs and neighborhoods of these two groups are rigidly segregated, and Latinos in many areas have accomplished their goal of driving out blacks. One study concluded, however, that the vast majority of victims in each group are killed by their own people. The study tracked killings in one Los Angeles neighborhood between 1994 and 2004 and found that 94 percent of African Americans were killed by other African Americans, and that 77 percent of Latinos were killed by other Latinos.

These days, Chris Bowers wakes up every morning to a vivid reminder that crossing borders can get you killed in South LA's [Los Angeles] Harbor Gateway area. Just outside the fence in front of his rented stucco house on Harvard Boulevard is a silver scooter, an assortment of dried flowers and a dozen candles bearing religious messages written in Spanish and English—a makeshift memorial to Cheryl Green, the 14-year-old whose murder last December [2006] by members of the 204th Street Gang sparked accusations of Latino "ethnic cleansing" of African-Americans. "There were two of them," says Bowers, a 22-year-old college student and high school football coach. "They came up and shot off one shot. They looked confused, and then shot off the rest of the rounds." Jonathan Fajardo, 18, and Ernesto Alcarez, 20, members of 204th Street, have been charged with gunning down Green as she stood with her scooter talking to friends. Police say they had been seeking a black person to kill.

After greeting a friend who drives by in a beat-up suburban, Bowers, whose dreads and ready smile give him a [Bob] Marleyesque air, looks south and says, "From 207th down, blacks and Latinos get along; people drink beer together, kids skate and play with other kids. You see black and Latino interracial kids. People kick it together. It's a real community."

Then he looks up the street toward the ramshackle Del Amo Market, one of the few stores on the twelve-block strip that is Harbor Gateway—an establishment that 204th Streeters forbid black people to enter. "But over there, that way, no," he says. "You don't really see many black people over there."

Though he gets along with most people on either side of the invisible line and has a Latina girlfriend, Bowers himself must be vigilant of those policing the racial borders up the street. "Even I don't go to the store," he says, "'cause I might get shot."

Blacks Versus Browns

Bowers and most African-Americans and Latinos living in Harbor Gateway and other poor neighborhoods that are home to LA's 700 gangs and 40,000 gang members—the largest concentration of gangs in the world—increasingly find themselves trapped as unwilling gladiators in a zero-sum, black-versus-brown game, one broadcast as if it were a sporting event.

In these graffiti-filled, job-emptied neighborhoods, and in the media, receptivity to simplistic race war rhetoric appears to grow in direct proportion to the speed and intensity with which globalization, migration and economic dislocation remake the City of Angels. The rise of Latino power in LA, most

Violence between African Americans and Hispanics is on the rise in Los Angeles, California. These police officers were stationed at Thomas Jefferson High School in L.A. in April 2005 in response to several brawls between over 100 African American and Hispanic students. AP Images.

recently displayed in the electoral victory of Mayor Antonio Villaraigosa in 2005 and the last year's [2006] 2 million-strong immigrant rights march downtown, has taken place just as the once-powerful African-American community has watched its numbers and influence rapidly dwindle. (LA's 428,000 African-Americans now account for less than 11 percent of the city's population.) In the minds of some African-Americans, Latinos, especially poor immigrants, have replaced white racism as the primary cause of the disappearance of LA's robust black middle class in once-great black suburbs like Compton, built on a foundation of industrial and government jobs and reflected in the election of black officials like Mayor Tom Bradley. Since the end of the Bradley era, after the '92 riots announced that everything and nothing had changed in black LA, many explanations for black displacement have arisen— some of which cast the ascendant Latino majority in a role formerly reserved for whites who fought the rise of black power.

"Latinos who happen to be gang members are trying to push African-Americans out of that [Harbor Gateway] area," says the Rev. Eric Lee, president of the LA office of the Southern Christian Leadership Conference, as he sits at a desk flanked by portraits of Malcolm X and Martin Luther King Jr. "This is more dangerous than what the Ku Klux Klan was doing. More dangerous because it's coming from people in the same socio-economic situation. The Harbor Gateway killings were based on racial, not gang-on-gang, violence." . . .

Killing One's Own

Lost in it all is a sad but fundamental fact of life in poor Los Angeles: Most violent crimes, most murders, most attempted murders, most gang killings are intraracial. In one of the most comprehensive studies of LA homicides to date, University of California, Irvine, researcher George Tita tracked 500 killings that occurred between 1999 and 2004 in the 77th Precinct, which covers an area north of Harbor Gateway and Watts and is one of the most violent precincts in the county. He found that 94 percent of African-Americans were killed by other African-Americans and 77 percent of Latinos there were killed by other Latinos. Tita says there is a recent "uptick" in racially motivated killings, "but it makes absolutely no sense to ignore all the other homicides because of these rare events."

A Problem Unsolved

Adam Nossiter

Adam Nossiter is a writer for the New York Times.

Thirteen years before the publication of Maya Angelou's I Know Why the Caged Bird Sings, *federal troops were sent into Little Rock, Arkansas (the setting of Angelou's book), to quell violence over racial desegregation in the area's schools. In 2007, fifty years after that event, racial discord continues as black parents clash with white parents and a black school superintendent. The central quarrel is over the superintendent's elimination of various nonteaching jobs that were held by blacks. Whites, who support the superintendent, point out the rise in test scores and enrollment during his tenure there. Some black parents privately report that he cares about the students and is a good manager.*

Fifty years after the epic desegregation struggle at Central High School [in Little Rock, Arkansas,] the school district here is still riven by racial conflict, casting a pall on this year's ambitious commemorative efforts.

In the latest clash, white parents pack school board meetings to support the embattled superintendent, Roy Brooks, who is black. The blacks among the school board members look on grimly, determined to use their new majority to oust him. Whites insist that test scores and enrollment have improved under the brusque, hard-charging Mr. Brooks; blacks on the board are furious that he has cut the number of office and other non-teaching jobs and closed some schools.

The fight is all the more disturbing to some here because it erupted just as a federal judge declared Little Rock's schools finally desegregated, 50 years after a jeering white mob massed outside Central High to turn back integration.

Racial Conflict in Schools

In 1957, the fight was over whether nine black students could attend an entirely white high school. Now it is over whether the city's black leaders can exert firm control over the direction and perquisites of an urban school district in the way that white leaders did for decades. When Mr. Brooks, who declined a request for an interview, cut 100 jobs, he saved money but earned the fierce ill will of many other blacks, who see the district as an important source of employment and middle-class stability.

Many whites, on the other hand, see the district, where issues of race have long been a constant backdrop, as a bloated bureaucracy, ripe for Mr. Brooks's pruning. Where some blacks say Mr. Brooks disregards them and cozies up to the white business establishment, many whites say he is merely trying to stop white flight.

The bitter racial split has left some residents questioning the dimensions of advancement in the intervening years. There are no mobs in the street this time, but the undercurrents are nasty.

"We're quite concerned about what kind of progress we have or haven't made," said Andre Guerrero, a white member of the Central High School 50th Anniversary Commission.

"This is a power struggle about whose voice is going to prevail," Mr. Guerrero said as the school board prepared to meet last week.

Mr. Brooks's tenure and the fight over him has thrown the district into turmoil.

"I've never seen anything like this—the divisiveness, the hate," said the leader of the teacher's union, Katherine Wright

Knight. Another outspoken critic, Katherine Mitchell, the board president, said, "I'm saying, we have really regressed." . . .

Other urban public school districts in the South have suffered through similar racial battles over leadership, aggravated by symptoms that prevail here, too: white flight, inner-city poverty and what is referred to as the "achievement gap," the wide divergence in test results between white and black students. The gap fuels resentment and makes an anathema of any perceived administrative leaning toward white students. . . .

Quality Versus Patronage

So polarized are the two sides that after Mr. Brooks summoned a statistician to demonstrate improvements in the schools at a recent board meeting, his opponents summoned another statistician to demonstrate precisely the opposite. Black and white board members took turns rolling their eyes and looking skeptical.

Jay P. Greene, head of the department of education reform at the University of Arkansas, said in an interview that Little Rock's scores had been improving, like scores around the state, though pushing them up in a troubled urban district "itself is an achievement."

The chamber of commerce backs Mr. Brooks, and the conservative editorial page of the *Arkansas Democrat-Gazette* crusades for him. Neither endorsement helps his image with black critics, who see his actions as inherently favoring whites.

He is "a person who doesn't identify with black people at all," said John Walker, a Little Rock civil rights lawyer who represents black students in the court case, which he has appealed. "The only thing he stands for is putting black people down."

Though many whites hail the cuts in administration—a legislative study found it "terribly bloated," a lawyer said—Ms. Mitchell, the board president, said of them angrily: "African-

The "Little Rock Nine" are escorted into Little Rock Central High School by U.S. Army soldiers as they desegregate the school on September 25, 1957. AFP/Getty Images.

American employees have lost $918,000," and she enumerated positions lost or downgraded. Many whites laud the closing of the three schools with low attendance.

Dr. Greene, of the University of Arkansas, said he feared that the dispute was really about patronage, not educational quality. "I think it would be hard to make strong criticisms of the superintendent on educational grounds," he said.

Mr. Brooks came from Orlando, Fla., three years ago, an administrator and former principal with a reputation for toughness and improving intractable schools, and he was opposed from the beginning by Ms. Mitchell and the teachers' union, whose leader immediately predicted he would fail. His fortunes went downhill when blacks achieved their historic majority on the board.

Mr. Brooks sat impassively through the recent board meeting, never making eye contact with his critics. They voted to send him a letter outlining why they wanted to be rid of him; on April 30 [2007] he sued the board president in federal court, saying she was intimidating potential witnesses who might testify for him at a likely administrative hearing over whether he should be dismissed.

Black parents remained largely silent at the board meeting. But several other black parents interviewed as they picked up their children at Dunbar Middle School were not following the board majority's line.

"He's a real hands-on superintendent," said Ray Webster, whose small boys were jumping up and down in the back seat. Mr. Webster had met Mr. Brooks through the parent-teacher association.

"He actually cares about the kids. He actually shows concern for the kids," he said, but that is a view vehemently rejected by his critics.

I Had a Dream

Bill Maxwell

*Bill Maxwell is a columnist, editorial writer, and editorial board
member for the* St. Petersburg Times. *He is also a former faculty member of the University of Illinois at Chicago and of
Northern Illinois University.*

*Journalist Bill Maxwell was intensely interested in higher educa-
tion for African Americans, especially at traditionally black colleges. Having been educated in an all-black college himself in the
1960s, Maxwell had faith in historically black colleges and universities, where closer attention could be given to African American students and their problems. In 2004 he took leave from his
job to teach at Stillman College, a traditionally black institution
in Tuscaloosa, Alabama. He found a devoted faculty, but only a
handful of competent and willing students.*

The August sun beat down and the temperature already
was approaching 80 degrees on Monday morning as I
neared Stillman College. This would be my first day as a professor at this small historically black school in Tuscaloosa, an
old Southern city of fewer than 80,000 residents where the
University of Alabama and the Crimson Tide football team
overshadow everything else. . . .

Suspicious Arrival

Driving my 13-year-old, un-air-conditioned Chevy Blazer past
the guard house, I became apprehensive when I noticed about
a dozen male students wearing baggy pants, oversized white
T-shirts, expensive sneakers and assorted bling standing
around shooting the breeze. At least two had "jailhouse tats"

on their arms, crude tattoos suggesting that these young men had spent time behind bars. They carried no books or anything else to indicate they were on a college campus.

I got a good look at their faces. I wanted to remember these young men if any of them showed up in my classes.

Behind them, several others sat on a low brick wall near the dorm entrance. They, too, were clad like extras in a gangsta rap video. It was a scene straight out of "the hood"— young black men seemingly without direction or purpose, hanging out on the corner. In this case, they were hanging out on what is popularly known as "The Yard" on a college campus where they were supposed to be preparing for a more productive life.

I had expected a more collegiate scene on Aug. 9, 2004. . . .

When I began my first day at Stillman, I was channeling my experiences of long ago. I would be a professor who would inspire and guide the lives of young black women and men who wanted to become successful journalists.

As it turned out, I would last just two years before returning to the [*St. Petersburg*] *Times*. I left the campus disheartened and disillusioned, and I regretted leaving behind a handful of dedicated students with real potential. Another graduating class has just left Stillman through the same gates I first entered in 2004, but I no longer feel welcome on campus. . . .

"Take Your Seats and Be Quiet!"

At 8 on that first morning, I met my freshman English class. I had volunteered to teach it because I wanted to assess the writing skills of the students in general. Because the chairman of my department had promised me small classes, I had expected no more than 15 students. Instead, I faced 33. All were black; more than half were women. Four of the men had been in front of King Hall earlier.

The room was noisy, and two who had been in front of King Hall were horsing around. I put my books on the table and raised an arm for silence. When only a few students paid attention I raised my arm again, and this time I yelled.

"All right, knock it off! Take your seats and be quiet!" . . .

"I Ain't Taking This Class"

That afternoon, I met my opinion writing and news writing/reporting classes. I had five students in one and seven in the other. Again, I called the roll and took writing samples. That night at home, I eagerly read the papers. These budding journalism majors were the reason I came to Stillman.

But after an hour of reading, I did not see how any of them would become reporters and editors without superhuman efforts on their part and mine. None had any sense of how a news article comes together. None knew how to write a compelling lead or how to use the active voice. Only one, a young woman in the opinion writing class, had written for a high school newspaper.

During the next class meetings, I returned the papers. I did not mark the work, but I explained the writing was disappointingly bad and that they would have to work overtime to learn to write at an acceptable level. All except the one student who had a decent essay were outraged.

"I thought this was going to be a real English class," a student said.

I asked her which high school she had attended and what she meant. The Selma High School graduate said her English teacher had let students spend most of their time discussing current events and writing short paragraphs. They wrote one essay all term. Most of the other students nodded approvingly. I did not tell the class that Selma High was considered to be academically inferior. I did tell them we would follow the syllabus, which required eight essays and four revisions. I also

115

told them they would have to complete the grammar quizzes in the textbook. Everyone, except the competent writer, groaned.

"I ain't taking this class," one of the students who had been in front of King Hall said. He stood, nodded to his three friends and walked out of the room. One of them followed. The other two stared at me and scowled for the remainder of the period.

The journalism students in the other two classes accepted my criticism without grumbling. In fact, they were pleased with the prospect of learning how to write "like real reporters," said Kristin Heard, a freshman from Montgomery....

Resisting Knowledge

After a week, I faced another problem that my seasoned colleagues knew well but failed to warn me about: Most Stillman students refuse to buy their required textbooks. I discovered the problem on a Friday when I met my English class to discuss the assigned essay in the text. They were to write an essay in response to the reading.

Only one student, the young man who wrote well, had read the essay. He had the text in front of him. The others had not purchased the text. I warned them that if they returned to class without their books, they would receive an F. But only five of 31 students brought their texts to the next class.

Most students had book vouchers as part of their financial aid, so I told those without books to walk with me to the bookstore, a distance of about three football fields. Some did not follow me, and I tried to remember who they were. At the store I watched students wander around, obviously trying to avoid buying the book. Only about eight wound up buying one.

I became angry that I had to deal with such a self-destructive, juvenile problem. I saw the refusal to buy the text as a collective act of defiance. I knew that if I lost this battle, I would not have any control in this class and no respect.

The next Monday, I went to class dreading a showdown. While calling the roll, I asked the students to show me their texts. Eighteen still did not have them. One said he had bought the book but left it in his dorm room "by mistake." I told him to go get it. He gathered his belongings and left. He never came to class again.

As promised, I recorded an F for all students who did not bring their texts. The last two young men from in front of King Hall walked out. I saw myself as having failed them as a professor, but I was relieved they were gone.

I also decided to take away students' excuses for not having access to the texts. I personally bought two copies of each book and put them on reserve in the library. From time to time, I would check to see who had used them. During the entire semester, the books were used only six times. . . .

An Ally at My Side

Lucinda Coulter was one of the bright lights at Stillman and an ally in the mission to groom young journalists. The professor, who is white, had a doctorate in American literature and had written for several magazines. She was a journalism instructor at the University of Alabama until she was hired at Stillman for a tenure-track position in 2000.

It wasn't an easy transition.

"During my first semester, I was overwhelmed with the workload," she told me during one of our gripe sessions. "I taught five classes and revitalized the student newspaper. The president had shut it down. It had become unprofessional. It looked like a yearbook instead of a newspaper.

"I was discouraged by the end of the year because of the workload. I returned the next year only because the faculty members in the English department were so supportive. We became close friends. We felt a common bond because we had a handful of genuinely wonderful kids."

We quickly developed a similar bond as we each taught about a dozen journalism students my first semester. Together we urged the students to read the *Tuscaloosa News*, which cost 50 cents, so we could discuss the news and how the newspaper approached it. But the newspaper had long ago removed its lone paper rack from Stillman's campus because of theft and vandalism. The nearest racks were several blocks away at two gas stations. None of our students would walk that far to buy the newspaper, and only a few would go online to read it.

"If you want to be a piano player," I often said in class, "you have to practice playing the piano. If you want to be a reporter, you have to read newspapers."

Hardly any students brought the newspaper to class. So Lucinda and I used our own money to buy each student a copy of the *Tuscaloosa News* every morning. The students repaid us for about three weeks, but when they stopped we kept buying it anyway. We knew some of them were living from hand to mouth. We also bought enough copies of the *New York Times*, the *Birmingham News* and *USA Today* for the students to share each day.

Newspapers weren't all we bought. Students at other college newspapers have plenty of camera equipment. We bought dozens of disposable cameras for students to take photographs to go along with their stories for the student newspaper, the *Tiger's Paw*. We changed the name to the *Advance*, a more mature-sounding name, during my second semester.

While many college newspapers are printed daily or weekly, we struggled to publish one edition each semester. Of the 12 students on the newspaper staff when I arrived, eight were English majors and only three had journalism experience in high school.

Few efforts in academia are tougher than trying to teach English majors how to write like journalists. English majors tend to believe that complicated prose and obfuscation are smart. Clear prose—the bread and butter of journalism—is considered unsophisticated and incapable of conveying deep thought and important ideas.

I had a hard time getting students to use short words instead of long ones: "ended" instead of "terminated;" "use" instead of "utilization;" "aim" instead of "objective."

Constance Bayne, a freshman from Tennessee, was an immediate exception. After I graded three of her stories, she had an epiphany during an individual grading session.

"I see what you mean," she said, studying my revision of one of her attempts at pomposity. "Yours is better. It's real easy to read."

"That's what we always want," I said. "Simplicity is elegant."

She smiled and read the rest of my revisions.

The Messages Were Lost

I tried my best to cultivate a love of language and reading. Two sayings were on my office door. One was a Chinese proverb: "It is only through daily reading that you refresh your mind sufficiently to speak wisely." The other came from me: "Being Smart is Acting Black."

But the messages were lost on students who had read so little growing up and had never acquired basic academic skills. I was not surprised to learn that only two of my students had read more than three of the books most high school students have read, books such as *Moby Dick, The Sun Also Rises, The Color Purple and Invisible Man.*

Those of us who were teaching the required general education courses—all of us from the nation's respected universities, such as the University of Chicago, Indiana University, the University of Florida and Princeton—had to face a harsh reality. We primarily were practicing remediation.

Every day in my classes, I reviewed basic grammar and showed students how to use the dictionary effectively, lessons normally taught in elementary and middle school.

Homework was another major problem. Writing courses, especially journalism courses, are labor intensive for students and the professors. Reporting—going into the field, interviewing sources, finding official records and verifying information for accuracy—is essential. After most of my students continued to hand in articles that had only one interview, I began requiring at least four interviews, with the sources' telephone numbers, for each story. Most of the students balked and continued to hand in work with an insufficient number of interviews.

Meeting deadlines, a must in journalism, was yet another problem. Few of my students regularly met the Monday deadline. I would deduct a letter grade for each day the copy was late. Some students received F's on all of their work. To avoid flunking them, I let them write in class.

But that required them to show up, and I seldom had all students present. Attending class seemed to be an inconvenience. The college had an official attendance policy, but few professors followed it strictly because most of our students would have flunked out before mid-term. On most days, I did not call the roll. I simply tried to remember who was present.

I recall the afternoon I sat alone in my room waiting for the seven students in the reporting class to show up. At 20 minutes past the hour, a white colleague peeked in and saw me in the otherwise empty room.

"You must've had a serious assignment due?" he said.

We had a big laugh. But it was a painful laugh.

"It's the Stillman way," he said. "A lot of these kids won't attend class, and, when they do, they walk in late. They're on CPT (Colored People's Time)."

Although I laughed with my colleague, I was ashamed that a white person so easily joked about CPT.

"They don't have intellectual curiosity," I said. "We weren't like that at Wiley or Bethune-Cookman."

"I know what you mean."

This time, we did not laugh. I gathered my books and newspapers, turned out the lights and left.

I hardly ever saw anyone take notes during lectures in the English class. Instead, I had to regularly chastise students for text messaging their friends and relatives and for going online to read messages and send messages. The college issued free laptops to all students who maintained a passing grade-point average.

When I confronted students about text messaging, I was met with hostility. I even had a few students leave class to make calls or send text messages. Two male students threatened to physically attack Lucinda and another female professor because they demanded that the students put away their laptops in class.

Each time, I would leave the English class exhausted, angry and sad. I would go home on many evenings during my first month wanting to cry, and things didn't get much better as the year progressed.

I had come to Stillman on the mission of my life: I wanted to be of use, to help "uplift the race" as my professors had taught me. But as my first school year ended in the spring, instead of feeling useful and as if I were helping to uplift the race, I was feeling helpless and irrelevant.

A Dream Lay Dying

Bill Maxwell

Bill Maxwell is a columnist, editorial writer, and editorial board member at the St. Petersburg Times. *He is also a former faculty member of the University of Illinois at Chicago and of Northern Illinois University.*

After completing his first year of teaching at Stillman College, journalist Bill Maxwell returns to the traditionally black school for his second year with trepidation and anxiety, even though his dream of establishing a viable journalism program had been decently funded and encouraged. The program fails from a lack of student participation, and Maxwell discovers that many of his students have hard lives, having to work all night with no time to study. Many have children or siblings to support. To make matters worse, the administration admits felons and parolees into the college and Maxwell learns some of his female students were afraid because an alleged rapist was allowed on campus.

After spending the summer trying to shake off the disappointment over my first year as a professor at Stillman College, I began the 2005 fall semester looking for even the smallest signs that I could make a difference in the lives of black students by setting high standards and inspiring them to rise to the challenge.

The first ray of hope that August morning came as I unlocked my office door and was greeted by Constance Bayne, my most diligent journalism student. The mere fact that she had bought her textbooks made me feel some degree of success. My first year, many students had refused to get the textbooks even when they had vouchers to cover the cost.

Constance's enthusiasm was reassuring, and I remember thinking that if I had 10 students like her I could transform the college into a place that attracted other high achievers from throughout Alabama. . . .

Students' Attitudes

During those first few weeks of school, the new equipment began arriving and my hopes continued to rise. My first year at Stillman, which had fewer than 1,000 students, had not been as smooth or as fulfilling as I had hoped. My students' academic performance had been generally disappointing, and I could not persuade most students to even attend class regularly.

Still, I believed that with a real newsroom we were ready to make significant progress. Before my arrival at Stillman, my colleague Lucinda Coulter had produced the student newspaper on her home computer without charging the college a dime. With a campus newsroom, we assumed that our students would begin to take the profession seriously and would love hanging out in their own space.

We soon learned that we had been naive. Nothing changed. Students rarely came to the newsroom except for classes. The majority preferred to socialize with their friends during their spare time, and others knew that one way to avoid an assignment for the newspaper was to avoid the newsroom where story leads and tips were posted on the bulletin board.

My colleagues and I were witnessing the result of low admission standards. Were we expecting too much of young people who scored poorly on the SAT, who were rarely challenged to excel in high school, who were not motivated to take advantage of opportunities to learn, who could not imagine where a sound education could take them? . . .

Hard Lives

During the fall semester, I would try to make eye contact with students and speak to them as we passed in the halls and on

The Yard, the grassy campus gathering spot. Very few of them would return my greetings. Most were sullen. But I also saw something more disturbing in their faces: Many of these young people were sad and unhappy. Very few smiled.

A colleague who had taught at Stillman for more than 10 years confirmed my observations. "Our kids haven't had many good things in their lives," she said. "Many of them are angry and negative and rude. They've had hard lives. Some of them don't belong here."

She was right. A number of students had criminal records, and others were awaiting trial on criminal charges. Stillman accepted them because they could not attend college anywhere else.

Terry Lee Brock, a 41-year-old freshman, was shot several times by a woman around 2 one morning in early February in front of the Night Stalker's Lounge. He died a short time later at the hospital. His trial for rape had been scheduled to begin the following week.

I did not learn until after his death that many of our female students were afraid of Terry. At least two told me they had complained to college officials that an alleged rapist was allowed on campus.

While we had students such as Terry who had no business being on a college campus, we went out of our way to help others who faced adversity and worked to overcome it.

"A lot of my students reared themselves and their sisters and brothers," Lucinda said. "They're adults before they're ready to be adults."

One of my students, a 25-year-old senior journalism major, grew up in several foster homes in different states. At Stillman, she had a part-time job, carried a full academic load and wrote for the student newspaper. She was an inspiration. When she graduated, I wrote a letter of recommendation that helped her land a public relations job in Atlanta. Her boss e-mailed me a few months later to say that my student was doing well and could stay with the firm as long as she wanted.

The college did not keep an accurate count, but we knew many young women on campus were mothers. One of my students was a 20-year-old mother of two pressed for time and money. But she had good attendance and turned in passable homework.

I met several students who had legally adopted their siblings. For one reason or another, their parents were temporarily or permanently absent. Some of my colleagues and I empathized and gave these students breaks, such as giving them take-home quizzes and exams and sometimes excusing them from class if they had written excuses from their employers. . . .

Instead of taking pride in being exemplary students, many were devotees of hip-hop culture. They were anti-intellectual, rude and profane.

I always was amazed that so many of the women tolerated the crude way the men spoke to them. One afternoon in my English class, a male student called a young woman "a big-assed ugly bitch." I expected her to slap him, and I would not have intervened. Instead, she dismissed the whole thing with a wave of her hand and turned to chat with her roommate. After class, I asked her about the insult.

"That fool don't mean nothing to me," she said. "He ain't nothing but a stupid brother from Anniston or somewhere."

The lesson was clear and disheartening: Personal insult, crude language and threatening behavior were a way of life for many students. I saw this kind of exchange repeated dozens of times in the classroom and on the Yard. I had no doubt that the influences of hip-hop contributed greatly to this ugly reality and other deleterious trends. . . .

The effects of poverty made teaching and learning arduous. I asked a student why she always fell asleep in my reporting and news writing class.

"I work full-time at Target at night," she said. "I can't get enough sleep."

I asked the obligatory questions: Why did she work so many hours? Did her family help her? What was she spending her money on? Did she have financial aid? Did she have a scholarship? Did she live on campus?

Her life's story was heartbreaking and yet typical of so many others. Born and reared in Selma, she was 19 years old. She had met her father once when she was 10. Her mother had been in and out of jail until her death in 1996 at age 34. Her then-64-year-old grandmother had assumed responsibility for her and her three siblings.

Although she had a student loan to help pay tuition, she had to pay for everything else and needed a car to get to work and to drive back to Selma. She also had to send money to her grandmother, who was living on Social Security and money from a part-time job as a caretaker for a disabled woman. Everyone except her grandmother said this teenager had no business attending college. Her place was in Selma with the rest of the family. . . .

Death of the Dream

In early October, Lucinda and I planned a field trip to Washington for the 10th anniversary celebration of the Million Man March. Learning often takes place outside the classroom, and we thought our students would benefit from being around thousands of other black Americans who would travel from across the country to the National Mall. They also would see how professional journalists cover a national news story.

We reserved a college van for the 800-mile drive from Tuscaloosa. Six students agreed to come, and Lucinda and I reserved several Washington hotel rooms on our personal credit cards. But the day before we were to leave, all but one student backed out and we canceled the trip. Once again, I was angry and disappointed.

This wasn't the first nor the last time many students would pass up an opportunity to escape the campus and learn something. . . .

While disagreeable staff members and financial red tape were constant irritants, nothing was more appalling than the students' disregard for college property.

During the spring semester, the Tuscaloosa Fire Department put out trash can fires in King Hall. I was angry and embarrassed to see a team of white firefighters trying to save a dormitory named for the Rev. Martin Luther King Jr. that black students had trashed.

"Why do they do this to their own buildings?" a white firefighter asked me.

I went inside the dorm to see the damage. Students had stuffed trash cans with paper and fabric and set them on fire. The smoke damage was enormous. The walls were blackened, the windows were smudged and the pungent smell of smoke lingered and stuck to everything.

Even without the fire damage, the place would have looked like a war zone. Holes had been kicked and punched in the walls. Windows were broken, floors were scarred and most of the furniture was damaged. The two dorms routinely underwent major repairs after each semester.

Two of my students, both journalism majors, were desperate to move out of King Hall. The last time I saw them, one had found an apartment and the other was looking for a place he could afford.

I've Wasted Two Years

By the end of the spring semester, I knew that I could not remain at Stillman another year. I had a few good students, but a few were not enough. One morning as I dressed for work, I accepted the reality that too much of my time was being wasted on students who did not care. I felt guilty about wanting to leave. But enough was enough.

A week before I left Stillman as a professor, I drove through the main gate en route to a final exam. As always, I saw a group of male students hanging out in front of King Hall.

The same four I had seen when I drove onto campus nearly two years earlier were milling about on the lawn. I parked my car and walked over to the group.

"Why don't you all hang out somewhere else?" I asked.

"Who you talking to, old nigger?" one said.

"You give the school a bad image out here," I said.

They laughed.

"Hang out somewhere else or at least go to the library and read a book," I said.

They laughed and dismissed me with stylized waves of the arm.

I walked back to my old Chevy Blazer, sad but relieved that I would be leaving.

In my office, I sat at my desk staring at a stack of papers to be graded. I'm wasting my time, I thought I've wasted two years of my professional life. I don't belong here.

I put the papers in a drawer. I did not read them. Why read them?

Family, Race, and Freedom

Larissa MacFarquhar

Larissa MacFarquhar is a staff writer for the New Yorker.

Barack Obama grew up moving from place to place, as Maya Angelou did, scarcely seeing his father and contending with his mother's insatiable appetite for adventure. The turbulence and instability of his family left him disillusioned. Yet, Obama made it to Harvard Law School, and his experience led him to believe that freedom is often just abandonment, and universalism is an illusion. Choices, he says, are not his alone. The past does impinge on the present.

What's strange about this is that the serene man his friends describe could not be more different from the person [Senator Barack] Obama himself describes in his memoir, *Dreams from my Father*. In that book, the young Obama is confused and angry, struggling to figure out who he is, often high, wary of both white condescension and black rage, never trusting himself, always suspicious that his beliefs are just disguised egotism, his emotions just symptoms of his peculiar racial lot. Of course, the book is about his emergence from this state of mind—it's a traditional tale of self-finding which ends, traditionally, with a wedding, in which his confusions are resolved—but the contrast between the Obama of the book and the Obama visible to the world is nonetheless so extreme as to be striking. "He was grounded, comfortable in his own skin, knew who he was, where he came from, why he believed things," Kenneth Mack, a friend of Obama's from Harvard and now a professor there, says. "When I read the book, I was surprised—the confusion and the anger that he described, maybe they were there below the surface, but they were not manifest at all." Asked about this, Obama says, "You know, what puzzles me is why people are puzzled by that."

The Angry Years

"That angry character lasts from the time I was fifteen to the time I was twenty-one or so. I guess my explanation is I was an adolescent male with a lot of hormones and an admittedly complicated upbringing. But that wasn't my natural temperament. And the book doesn't describe my entire life. I could have written an entirely different book, about the joys of basketball and what it's like to bodysurf as the sun's going down on a sandy beach."

Why didn't he write a book about the joys of basketball? Why focus on an aspect of himself that seems so politically unpalatable? When Obama was in law school, just before he wrote *Dreams*, he talked about wanting to be mayor of Chicago, and since people tend for some reason to tolerate—indeed, to delight in—considerably more eccentricity and dubious conduct in mayors than they do in other elected officials, it may be that he wrote the book with that ambition in mind. He probably realized that revealing his druggy past was the best way to defuse the issue in the future. But Obama is a master storyteller, and it's likely that he also knows that the typical story of the political candidate—doing very well in school, followed by doing very well in a profession, meanwhile relishing a good life (victory, revenge, nice house, basketball, whatever)—is not moving or inspiring stuff.

When he was working as a community organizer in Chicago, Obama spoke to a number of black ministers, trying to persuade them to ally themselves with his organization, and in the course of these conversations he discovered that most had something in common. "One minister talked about a former gambling addiction," he writes. "Another told me about his years as a successful executive and a secret drunk. They all mentioned periods of religious doubt ... the striking bottom and shattering of pride; and then finally the resurrection of self, a self alloyed to something larger. That was the source of their confidence, they insisted: their personal fall, their subsequent redemption. It was what gave them the authority to preach the Good News." Cassandra Butts, a friend of Obama's from law school, remembers, "Barack used to say that one of his favorite sayings of the civil-rights movement was 'If you cannot bear the cross, you can't wear the crown.'"

Obama rose to prominence at the 2004 Democratic Convention, describing his life as a celebration of the American dream: a "skinny kid with a funny name," the product of an improbably idealistic union between an African man and a girl from Kansas, he rose out of obscurity to attend Harvard Law School and would go on—it was by then clear—to become the third black U.S. senator since Reconstruction. But in another sense his life runs directly counter to the American dream, rejecting the American dreams of his parents and grandparents, in search of something older.

Roots

Obama's maternal grandfather, Stanley Dunham, grew up a small-time delinquent in El Dorado, Kansas. He didn't know what he wanted to do with himself, but he knew that he wanted to get out of Kansas—out of his parents' house, away from the airless parochialism of the small-town Midwest, where, as his grandson imagined it, "fear and lack of imagination choke your dreams so that you already know on the day that you're born just where you'll die and who it is that'll bury you." After a few false starts and eloping with a restless girl, he did what men of his type iconically do: he moved west. He moved to California, then to Seattle, and then, finally, to the last frontier, as far west as he could go without ending up east again, to Hawaii.

From a starting point eight thousand miles farther east, in Kenya, Obama's other grandfather, Hussein Onyango, moved in the same direction for similar reasons. Discontented and ambitious, he left his father's village, curious about the new white people settling in a nearby town. He took to wearing European clothing and adopted European notions about hygiene and property with a convert's fervor. During the Second World War, he travelled to Europe as a cook for the British Army.

The children of these two men, Obama's parents, one generation removed from their native places, were freer than their fathers. Obama's mother, Ann, married first a man from Kenya and then, when that man left, a man from Indonesia, and when the second marriage fell apart, she briefly returned home to Hawaii to start a master's in anthropology, and then left again for Indonesia, to spend several years doing field work. She gave her son, then thirteen, the choice whether to come with her or stay behind at his school in Hawaii, and he chose to stay.

Obama's father was expelled from school, and his father cut him off, but he managed to obtain a scholarship to attend college in America. He left his pregnant wife and his son to study econometrics at the University of Hawaii. There he met Ann Dunham, married her, and had another child, Barack. He left his second family to return to Kenya to work for the government, where he married another American woman and had two more children with her. After a few years, this third family disintegrated, and, because he was unwilling to accept the unfairness of Kenya's persistent tribalism, so did his government position. Angry and penniless, he started to drink.

Story of a Family

"What strikes me most when I think about the story of my family," Obama writes, "is a running strain of innocence, an innocence that seems unimaginable, even by the measures of

Senator Barack Obama (D-Ill.) announces his candidacy for president of the United States in 2007. AP Images.

childhood." Innocence is not, for him, a good quality, or even a redeeming excuse: it is not the opposite of guilt but the opposite of wisdom. In Obama's description of his maternal grandfather, for instance, there is love but also contempt. "His was an American character, one typical of men of his generation, men who embraced the notion of freedom and individualism and the open road without always knowing its price," Obama writes. "Men who were both dangerous and promising precisely because of their fundamental innocence; men prone, in the end, to disappointment." Stanley Dunham's restlessness didn't get him anywhere but far away. He ended up an incompetent, unhappy insurance salesman, his life not very different from the one he might have lived if he'd stayed in Kansas, except that, having travelled all that distance to end up there, he was all the more dissatisfied with it. His daughter saw his dissatisfaction but learned the wrong lesson: the trouble wasn't that he had wandered in a meaningless fashion, wandering for wandering's sake, expecting that a new place meant a new life; the trouble was that he hadn't wandered far enough. She would go farther. "It was this desire of his to obliterate the past, this confidence in the possibility of making the world from whole cloth," Obama writes, "that proved to be his most lasting patrimony."

Obama's mother is, in his portrayal, an American innocent out of Henry James: a young girl who ventures into the world believing that things are as they seem to be; that a person's story begins when she is born and her relations with other people begin when she meets them; that you can leave your home without fear of injury or loneliness because people everywhere are more or less alike. She had no idea what she was getting into when she left Hawaii—no idea that only months before she arrived Indonesia had suffered a failed but brutal coup and the killing of several hundred thousand people. Eventually, somebody told her what had happened, but the knowledge didn't change her. "In a land where fatalism remained a necessary tool for enduring hardship," Obama writes, "she was a lonely witness for secular humanism, a soldier for

New Deal, Peace Corps, position-paper liberalism." She had a faith, inherited from her father and resistant to experience, "that rational, thoughtful people could shape their own destiny." She should have counted herself lucky for emerging from the experience with only a second divorce and two bewildered children. "Things could have turned out worse," her son wrote. "Much worse."

Innocence, freedom, individualism, mobility—the belief that you can leave a constricting or violent history behind and remake yourself in a new form of your choosing—all are part of the American dream of moving west, first from the old country to America, then from the crowded cities of the East Coast to the open central plains and on to the Pacific. But this dream, to Obama, seems credulous and shallow, a destructive craving for weightlessness. When Obama, as a young man, went to Kenya for the first time and learned how his father's life had turned out—how he had destroyed his career by imagining that old tribalisms were just pettiness, with the arrogant idea that he could rise above the past and change his society by sheer force of belief—Obama's aunt told him that his father had never understood that, as she put it, "if everyone is family, no one is family." Obama found this striking enough so that he repeated it later on, in italics: *If everyone is family, no one is family.* Universalism is a delusion. Freedom is really just abandonment. You might start by throwing off religion, then your parents, your town, your people and your way of life, and when, later on, you end up leaving your wife or husband and your child, too, it seems only a natural progression.

Reversing Escape

So when it came time for Obama to leave home he reversed what his mother and father and grandparents had done: he turned around and moved east. First back to the mainland, spending two years of college in California, then farther, to New York. He ended up in Chicago, back in the Midwest, from which his mother's parents had fled, embracing everything they had escaped—the constriction of tradition, the weight of history, the provincial smallness of community, settling for your whole life in one place with one group of people. He embraced even the dirt, the violence, and the narrowness that came with that place, because they were part of its memory. He thought about the great black migration to Chicago from the South, nearly a century before, and the traditions the migrants had made there. "I made a chain between my life and the faces I saw, borrowing other people's memories," he wrote. He wanted to be bound.

Of course, in a sense, by choosing to leave his family and move to a place to which he had no connection, he was doing exactly what his parents had done, but, unlike them, he decided to believe that his choosing self had been shaped by fate and family. There was, at least, something organic, something inescapable about that. "I can see that my choices were never truly mine alone," he wrote, "and that is how it should be, that to assert otherwise is to chase after a sorry sort of freedom." Choosing was the best that he could do. In time, the roots would grow. He married Michelle Robinson, a woman who already owned the memories and the roots, who was by birth the person he was trying to become: the child of an intact, religious black family from the South Side. He took a job organizing a South Side community that was disintegrating but that he hoped, through work and inspiration, to revive. Later, rejecting the agnosticism of his parents and his own skeptical instincts, he became a Christian and joined a church. "I came to realize," he wrote in his second book, *The Audacity of Hope*, that "without an unequivocal commitment to a particular community of faith, I would be consigned at some level to always remain apart, free in the way that my mother was free, but also alone in the same ways that she was ultimately alone."

By the time he arrived at law school, when he was twenty-seven, he had become the man he had imagined. All his life, people had considered him black because he looked black, however confused he might be inside, and now he was no longer confused. His conversion was complete. "If you had met him, you would never get that he was biracial," Kenneth Mack says. "You would never get that he grew up in Hawaii. When I met him, he just seemed like a black guy from Chicago. He seemed like a Midwestern black man."

For Further Discussion

1. Analyze the symbols in *I Know Why the Caged Bird Sings*, giving special attention to the title. (See Didion, Fox-Genovese, and Smith.)

2. Discuss the various aspects of maintaining black traditions. What about it is positive and what is negative? Do any of these traditions derive from slavery? Compare the old traditions with the new. (See Bloom, Fox-Genovese, Russell, and McPherson.)

3. Identify the racist encounters that occur in the novel. Are there similar encounters occurring in the twenty-first century? (See Hagen, Lupton, Arensberg, and Lovato.)

4. Discuss the relevance of the novel to the civil rights struggle. (See Bloom, Braxton, Walker, and Als.)

5. The matriarchy plays a critical part of Angelous's life, as it does in the lives of so many African American children. Discuss Angelou's ambivalence toward her strong grandmother. (See Bloom, Braxton, Didion, Smith, and Hagen.)

6. Discuss the effect Angelou's mother and father had on her life.

For Further Reading

Maya Angelou   *Gather Together in My Name.* New York: Random House, 1974.

Maya Angelou   *Singin' and Swingin' and Gettin' Merry Like Christmas.* New York: Bantam Books, 1977.

Maya Angelou   *The Heart of a Woman.* New York: Random House, 1981.

Maya Angelou   *All God's Children Need Traveling Shoes.* New York: Random House, 1986.

Gwendolyn Brooks   *Blacks.* Chicago: David, 1987.

Lorraine Hansberry *To Be Young, Gifted and Black: Lorraine Hansberry in Her Own Words.* Adapted by Robert Nemiroff. Englewood Cliffs, NJ: Prentice-Hall, 1969.

Zora Neale Hurston *Dust Tracks on a Road.* Philadelphia: Lippincott, 1942.

Jamaica Kincaid   *Annie John.* London: Picador, 1985.

Toni Morrison   *The Bluest Eye.* London: Chatto and Windus, 1979.

Toni Morrison   *Beloved.* London: Chatto and Windus, 1987.

Alice Walker   *The Color Purple.* London: Women's Press, 1983.

Patricia J.
Williams

The Alchemy of Race and Rights. London: Virago, 1991.

Bibliography

Books

Joanne Braxton, ed.	*Maya Angelou's I Know Why the Caged Bird Sings: A Casebook.* New York: Oxford University Press, 1999.
Stephen Butterfield	*Black Autobiography in America.* Amherst: University of Massachusetts Press, 1974.
Hazel Carby	*Reconstructing Womanhood: The Emergence of the Afro-American Woman Novelist.* New York: Oxford University Press, 1987.
Angela Davis	*Women, Race & Class.* London: Women's Press, 1982.
Jeffrey Elliot, ed.	*Conversations with Maya Angelou.* Jackson: University of Mississippi Press, 1989.
Mari Evans, ed.	*Black Women Writers (1950–1980): A Critical Evaluation.* Garden City, NY: Anchor Press, 1984.
Dolly McPherson	*Order Out of Chaos.* New York: Peter Lang, 1990.

Periodicals

Africa News Service	"Fight Against Black Racism Futile Without Tackling Stereotypes," January 4, 2005.

Carol Benson   "Out of the Cage and Still Singing," *Writer's Digest*, 1975.

Tokumbo Bodunde   "The Female Experience of Racism," *People's Weekly World*, March 10, 2007.

Shirley J. Cordell   "The Black Woman: A Focus on 'Strength of Character' in *I Know Why the Caged Bird Sings*," *Virginia English Bulletin* 36, no. 2 (Winter 1986).

Ebony   "Black Women Firsts: Pioneers in the Struggle for Racial and Gender Equality," March 1994.

Onita Estes-Hicks   "The Way We Were: Precious Memories of the Black Segregated South," *African American Review* 25, no. 1 (Spring 1993).

Susan Gilbert   "Maya Angelou's *I Know Why the Caged Bird Sings*: Paths to Escape," *Mount Olive Review* 1, no. 1 (Spring 1987).

Marita Golden   "White Women at Work: Successful Black-Women Executives Tell How They Confront 'White-Girl Privilege' on the Job—and Win!" *Essence*, October 2002.

G. Goodman Jr.   "Maya Angeou's Lonely Black Outlook," *New York Times*, March 24, 1972.

Edward Guthmann — "'We Are Being Injured Daily by Racism': African American Women Speak Out over Insults from Imus," *San Francisco Chronicle*, April 16, 2007.

Ernece B. Kelly — *"I Know Why the Caged Bird Sings,"* *Harvard Educational Review* 40, no. 4 (November 1970).

George E. Kent — "Maya Angelou's *I Know Why the Caged Bird Sings* and Black Autobiographical Tradition," *Kansas Quarterly* 7, no. 3 (Summer 1975).

Kenneth Kinnamon — "Call and Response," *Studies in Black American Literature* 2 (1996).

Lucinda H. MacKethan — "Mother Wit: Humor in Afro-American Women's Autobiography," *Studies in American Humor* 4, no. 2 (Spring 1985).

Myra K. McMurry — "Role-Playing as Art in Maya Angelou's *Caged Bird*," *South Atlantic Bulletin* 41, no. 2 (May 1976).

Frank Lamont Phillips — "Gather Together in My Name," *Black World* 24 (July 1975).

James Robert Saunders — "Breaking Out of the Cage," *Hollins Critic* 28, no. 4 (October 1991).

Marion M. Tangum and Margory Smelstor — "Hurston's and Angelou's Visual Art," *Southern Literary Journal* 31, no. 4 (Fall 1998).

Mary Vermillion — "Reimbodying the Self," *Biography* 15, no. 3 (Summer 1991).

Diane Weathers   "Black America's Dirty Little Secrets:
                   We've Fought as a Community
                   Against Racism. Now Two Noted
                   Scholars Say It's Time to Fight for
                   Respect from Our Men," *Essence*, July
                   2003.

Index

A

Abandonment, 33–35, 86–87
Acting career, 26
Africa, 83–84
African American children, racial self-hatred in, 86–87
African American church, 10, 58
African American literature, 69–70
African Americans
    exploitation of, 9–10
    injustices against, 95–97
    lack of job opportunities for, 10–11
    stereotypes of, 61
    white violence against, 91–92
African American women. *See* Black women
Agricultural labor, 10
All God's Children Need Traveling Shoes (Angelou), 83–84
Als, Hilton, 99
Andrew, William J., 35–36
Angelou, Maya
    autobiographies of, 16–17, 16–24, 81–83
    childhood of, 17–21, 43–44
    chronology of, 12–14
    civil rights movement and, 22–23, 26, 101–102
    honors received by, 25–26
    life of, 16–24
    See also works by
Anger, 27
Archetypes, 59
Arensberg, Liliane K., 85
Aspirations, 46
Athletics, 46–47

The Audacity of Hope (Obama), 136
Autobiographies
    Black, 52–53, 61, 63, 70–72
    motives for writing, 26
    See also Slave narratives; *specific works*

B

Bambara, Toni Cade, 100
Baxter, Vivian, 17
    abandonment by, 33–34, 86–87
    influence of, 23
    life with, 19–21, 40–41, 97
    use of humor by, 58
Bayne, Constance, 119, 122
Beauty, whiteness and, 43–44, 50–52, 54, 91
Benson, Carol, 76
Black autobiography, 52–53, 61, 63, 70–72
Black Boy (Wright), 53
Black colleges, 113–128
Black community, displacement of, 54–55
Black culture, 10, 17, 19, 42, 64–65, 80–81, 89–90
Black feminist writing, 100–101
Black heroism, 73
Black liberation art, 63
Black literature, 18
Black power movement, 72
Black women
    in *Caged Bird*, 63–64, 66
    motherhood and, 65–66
    as others, 26